TOPGUN LESSONS FROM THE SKY

U.S. NAVY PILOTS

FLETCHER MCKENZIE

SSP

This edition published 2023 by Squabbling Sparrows Press

ISBN 978-0-9951421-9-0 (Paperback)
ISBN 978-1-9911576-0-7 (Ebook)

A catalogue record for this book is available from the National Library of New Zealand.

Published by Squabbling Sparrows Press
PO Box 4213, Marewa, Napier 4143
New Zealand

Squabbling Sparrows Press

ALSO BY FLETCHER MCKENZIE

LESSONS FROM THE SKY

STORIES & LESSONS FROM
TOPGUN AIRCRAFT & CREW FROM THE U.S. NAVY

Dedicated to Art Scholl

Blue skies

54 year old film stunt pilot Art Scholl died during the production of the 1986 Top Gun movie. Flying his Pitts S-2 camera plane, he failed to recover from a flat spin and was lost in the Pacific Ocean. Neither Art nor his aircraft were ever found, so the exact cause of the crash was never able to be determined.

"**Even on a flight that we've seemingly done a hundred times, there are things that will always be out of the ordinary. It is paramount to discuss and remain vigilant to better combat it when the rotors start turning.**"
    LT Justine Engel
    U.S. Navy

CONTENTS

FOREWORD

"Aviation in itself is not inherently dangerous. But to an even greater degree than the sea, it is terribly unforgiving of any carelessness, incapacity or neglect."
Captain A. G. Lamplugh

In 1931, Captain Lamplugh was chief underwriter and principal surveyor of the British Aviation Insurance Company and, in that context, his assertion made sense. After all, man had been plying the seas for centuries and they understood the hazards of doing so. Powered flight, however, was in its relative infancy. They accepted that aircraft took off from terra firma and later returned there as well. It is little wonder that such returns would come to be known as landings.

But as far back as 20 years prior, audacious pilots had already begun mixing the sea and air in ways the good captain may not have fully appreciated. When Eugene Ely became the first American pilot to launch and recover aboard converted warships, he ushered in a new era of aviation - naval aviation - which would forever change warfare.

Mere decades after Ely's barnstorming-esque feats, launching and recovering propeller-driven combat aircraft at sea became not only routine, but pivotal to the outcome of World War II in the Pacific. Today, the act of hurling a 40,000-pound, fuel- and explosive-laden, aluminium and composite jet at a hulking 90,000-ton steel, nuclear-powered aircraft carrier is commonplace. And is likely occurring on one or more of the seven seas at this very moment. What has not changed over time, however, is the risk.

Make no mistake, naval aviation is dangerous.

Human error, material failure and environmental conditions are among the factors most attributable to aviation mishaps. These challenges are magnified one hundred-fold at sea. Imagine an airfield's-worth of people scurrying around a chaotic 4.5-acre flight deck complete with complex mechanical contraptions to launch and recover. Then add the environmental conditions. In addition to the usual weather hazards of thunderstorms, icing and fog—to name a few—pilots must also contend with a runway pitching up and down at the whims of an angry sea.

I spent over three years at sea during five aircraft carrier deployments, but it wasn't until my fourth deployment that nobody crashed an airplane. On my first deployment, two F/A-18 Hornets collided while joining on an aerial refuelling tanker at night, killing a 16-year veteran pilot and father of two.

On my second deployment, an S-3 Viking crashed moments after leaving the catapult. I watched in shock as two friends perished.

On my third deployment, an EA-6B Prowler caught fire after launch. Mercifully, all four occupants ejected to safety.

Between deployments, my air wing, and many others, suffered cold cats, parted wires, ramp strikes, OCF, CFITs, and a host of other mishaps so frequent that naval aviators have their own vernacular for them.

The hazards are there every single day, and they are real.

Sure, abiding by established policies and procedures is a good start. But it is the ready room retelling of near misses, close calls, and other "sea stories" that equips junior pilots to handle the myriad of risks. As a new pilot, I remember listening to stories from senior pilots. The stories usually began with "there I was..." before explaining some new way they cheated certain death and destruction.

One night on my first deployment, I was watching the ship's closed-circuit television - *Danger TV*, we called it. Our squadron executive officer was next to land. His aircraft was "coupled up", meaning the autopilot was flying as it followed a homing beacon from the ship for a theoretically perfect landing. I almost quit watching because coupled passes are typically not as colourful as manually flown passes. But as the XO's aircraft approached the back of the ship, I noticed the aircraft pitch up slightly and then nose over—a potentially disastrous turn.

On the flight deck, at the back of the ship, also observing the landing was the team of landing signal officers—pilots whose collateral duties were ensuring the safe and expeditious recovery of aircraft. They did not miss a beat, waving off the XO who overrode the autopilot to miss the back of the ship and sure disaster.

After recovering on the next pass, the XO, LSOs and curious onlookers like me debriefed the incident, watching and re-watching the Danger TV recording I had seen live. The XO explained what he experienced in the cockpit; the LSOs described what they observed from their vantage. They later voiced their concerns to headquarters, and the ship was told to do no more such coupled approaches until the carrier suitability team of test pilots could come out and investigate.

This experience, as well as the hours of sitting around sharing stories–first listening as a young pilot, later telling my own as a more seasoned aviator–was invaluable. In fact, they formalised this fleet-wide practice into a periodical known as Approach Magazine which, to this day, widely disseminates such lessons learned throughout the fleet for the benefit of all pilots.

Fletcher has assembled a version of that here. On the pages that follow are harrowing and unbelievable sea stories from the ranks of naval aviators with hundreds of years of cumulative experience. While you may never land a high-performance jet on an aircraft carrier (perhaps some of you might), you can still internalise the lessons shared on these pages as "best practices" to learn from others.

Because both sides are correct: aviation is terribly unforgiving of mistakes and naval aviation is inherently dangerous. Let these stories not only offer you a glimpse into the naval aviator's world but entertain and educate you to be a professional and safe pilot. You owe it to yourself and the generation that follows.

E. Vincent 'Jell-O' Aiello
TOPGUN Instructor
www.fighterpilotpodcast.com

Vincent attended his first airshow at eight years old. He earned a commission into the U.S. Navy after participating in the Navy Reserve Officer Training Corps program at the University of California, graduating with a degree in Applied Mathematics.

He spent the next 25 years flying all models of the F/A-18 Hornet and Super Hornet, the F-16A/B Fighting Falcon, the TA-4J Skyhawk, and other training aircraft. As an instructor at the Navy's fabled Fighter Weapons School, better known as TOPGUN, he accrued 3,800 flight hours and 705 day and night carrier landings over five aircraft carrier deployments, plus a deployment on the ground in Afghanistan.

After retiring from active duty, Vincent went on to a career with a major airline and is the founder and host of the Fighter Pilot Podcast, the internet radio show exploring the fascinating world of air combat: the aircraft, the weapons systems, and the people.

INTRODUCTION

**"There's no point to writing all this if there were
not lessons to be learned."**
CDR Cade Hines
U.S. Navy

Safety. No one dreams of flying in the Navy because it's a safe
occupation.

I asked some of my former squadron mates what started them on
the path to fly Navy jets. Several talked of seeing the power and
precision of the Blue Angels or Thunderbirds at airshows. Others
saw the films and posters shown at Naval Aviation recruiting booths,
drawn to the challenge and excitement they represented. The stories
of a college professor who had flown Navy fighters as a young man
stirred another friend.

Not one of them mentioned longing to fly for the safety factor.

In my case, my parents influenced me by taking me to air shows
when I was young. Somewhere around the age of 10 or 12, I latched

on to the idea of becoming a fighter pilot. I don't recall the exact circumstances, but once this idea took root, flying became my unchanging goal. I drew pictures of fighter jets and read books about them, absorbing every detail, imagining the almost limitless power, zooming among clouds and living in three dimensions.

My dreams didn't include checklists, boldface procedures and safety stand-downs.

In college, I took Navy ROTC (Reserve Officer Training Corps) and continued on the path to flying, but my eyesight went bad, so I could not become a fighter pilot. Pilots had to have 20/20 vision and I couldn't get LASIK surgery in the 1970s. I spent a few unpleasant months fretting over my future, but soon realised I could become a back-seater in a Navy fighter: the muscular F-4 or the incredible new F-14. And it all worked out. I did my part, invested my time and energy, and the Navy designated me a Radar Intercept Officer (RIO) in the F-14 Tomcat.

After that, I began living among the clouds. Studying energy manoeuvrability and missile launch parameters, tracking bandits on my radar and backing up my pilot on night carrier landings. I wore a g-suit to work and breathed 100% oxygen force-fed at positive pressure. The reality was much more than my youthful dreams ever conjured.

But I also abided by dozens of checklists, followed carefully developed procedures and then revised when found deficient, and took tests where a letter-perfect answer sheet was the requirement to pass. Among the millions of unfamiliar words I learned was the snappy acronym NATOPS - Naval Air Training and Operating Procedures Standardisation, a comprehensive program that affected every aspect of squadron life and all the Navy's flying and flight-related activity.

Naval aviation in the 1980s was a world where we routinely took risks that would make some people nervous. Or worse. When we were practising dogfighting, we sometimes flew within 500 feet of the opponent. Closer passes were a reason to end the engagement—the radio call was, "Knock it off"—to comply with the training tules that managed risk and increased safety margins of this dangerous activity: realistic training for air-to-air combat.

Although Navy fighter squadrons were home-based at naval air stations with long runways, we prepared for 7-month deployments aboard aircraft carriers by going aboard the carrier for training periods of several weeks. We flew day and night, using the carrier's powerful catapult like a slingshot to launch us from the flight deck and catching the arresting cable when we returned. The arresting cable wasn't as dramatic as the catapult, but mechanically it was just as impressive, slowing a 26-ton F-14 from 150 mph to zero in about two-seconds. For carrier operations, the flight deck was crowded with dozens of aircraft, hundreds of people, fuel hoses, small vehicles and live bombs and missiles. The Navy required a safety culture to perform these operations on a routine basis and to respond to emergencies.

Yes, there were emergencies. Off the coast of San Diego, and EA-6B Prowler loses an engine during the catapult shot. Senior officers confer and decide not to risk a shipboard recovery. They divert the jet to one of those land bases. An F-14 experiences a problem with its landing gear, and again they decide to divert.

Wise decisions. The nature of operations didn't require the aircraft to return to the carrier, and the risk of an accident ("mishap" in our lingo) was reduced by using a runway. We took plenty of risks during training, we reduced them when we could.

Months later, the carrier was in the middle of the Indian Ocean, where there was no realistic option to divert to a runway, and all of our maintenance technicians and tools were on the carrier. When a malfunction happened during the deployment, the aircraft had to return to the carrier. In many cases there was time to work the problem, so the pilot (and other crew if a multi-place aircraft) got on the radio with squadron representatives and carrier air operations personnel. They referred to NATOPS procedures, to their training and experience—all founded in the safety culture—to handle the situation with the least potential risk to people and machinery. If there was no time to decide, the aircrew used these same resources to guide their immediate actions. And after the smoke cleared, figuratively or literally, all available information was gathered and analysed, and we fed any lessons into the Navy's safety system for the benefit of others.

And then it's time to get ready for the next launch. In my squadrons, the briefer always included safety considerations, and we usually had a safety question of the day. Culture of safety.

These conditions applied not only to carrier aviation, but to all the Navy and Marine Corps flying machines, including patrol planes, transports and others. The safety culture and many concepts from aviation also spread to the rest of the Navy, although I have to figure that nuclear-powered submariners had a pretty good handle on safety by the time the aviation community got serious about it. And safety, of course, became of concern for all military services.

Where did this all come from? An excellent book on U.S. naval aviation safety, Gear Up, Mishaps Down, tells that story. Written by former combat pilot and commander of the Naval Safety Centre, Vice Admiral Robert F. Dunn, USN (Ret.), the book recounts the painful realisation by naval aviation leaders that they had a problem.

In 1954, naval aviation lost 536 people and 776 aircraft in 2,213 major mishaps. Although it could boast a proud combat record in World War II and Korea, naval aviation was in crisis through its high mishap rate. Through years of candid self-appraisal and a series of effective programs, the Navy lowered its aviation mishap rate and in 1999, the lowest year reported in this book, reported 9 deaths and 23 aircraft destroyed. A famous graph shows the dramatic progress.

I benefitted from it all, but was fortunate to have a glimpse of the wild past. When I went through the F-14 training squadron (aircraft-specific training squadrons were one part of the safety turnaround), some of our instructor pilots and RIOs had flown in the early 1960s and many had Vietnam experience. On rare days when they cancelled flying due to weather—it was San Diego, after all—dozens of instructors and students crowded into the small coffee mess and the instructors told stories. I loved listening to their tales of wild adventures: drinking and driving, smoking while flying, or performing other aviating stunts that left all of us thinking, "They were lucky to survive!"

But survive they did, becoming adherents to the safety culture and active promoters of it. They instilled in us impressionable youngsters respect for the dangers that were the constant companion of any person who defied gravity. They insisted we practice the hard-learned lessons that helped the Navy accomplish that incredible reduction in mishaps.

Did that transform flying into a dull exercise comprising rote procedures and endless checklists? Well, we were still flying Mach-2 capable Tomcats from aircraft carriers day and night. We were still training for combat, sometimes with four fighters opposed by eight or more adversaries in swirling dogfights. We were still practising low-level reconnaissance missions a few hundred feet above the ground, flying eight hundred feet per second. No, when it became safer, Naval Aviation did not become dull.

A few years after those rainy days, I was a TOPGUN instructor at the Navy Fighter Weapons School. Besides developing and training fighter tactics, we remained committed to safety. During a one-versus-one training dogfight, an adversary aircraft flew so close under my jet that I reflexively lifted my feet so his tail wouldn't hit them. There was no collision. He somehow missed us, but my pilot tersely called, "Knock it off. RTB". Return to base. During the first fifteen minutes of the debrief, my red-faced instructor pilot admonished the student adversary for his dangerous manoeuvre.

No, naval aviation was never dull.

For me, it was the inspiration to write several books that capture the excitement and commitment, as well as the occasional mishap and misadventure. In fact, a complete chapter of my first book, *TOPGUN Days*, details the story of my ejection during a carrier landing mishap. (Spoiler alert: the pilot and I both survived, and our

F-14 sank.) My most recent book, *Tomcat RIO*, includes several more, ahh, opportunities to learn lessons...

I think I made my point about dreaming of safe flying. I would also add that few read books about aviation safety. And yet, you have one in front of you. The aviation action and the inspiring resourcefulness of the pilots and aircrews will not disappoint you. It will not be dull, and if you learn a thing or two, that's even better.

Dave 'Bio' Baranek
TOPGUN Instructor
www.TopgunBio.com

Dave received his Wings of Gold as a RIO in 1980, then completed training for the F-14, and joined his first fighter squadron in April 1981. He was based at NAS Miramar in San Diego and deployed to the Pacific and Indian oceans. After joining VF-24, he received the callsign "Bio," which his former squadron mates still call him.

A TOPGUN air-to-air combat instructor in 1985, he flew aerial sequences used in the film Top Gun. He was also the dialogue advisor on the project. He experienced face-offs against Iranian forces in the 1980s, undertaking combat air patrols above hostile Iraq in the 1990s, and had command of an F-14 Tomcat squadron of 300 people. "Bio" enjoyed a successful and satisfying 20-year career in the Navy. He retired in 1999, and now works as a defence contractor.

PROLOGUE

"As a former TOPGUN instructor, I relished moments such as these where I had the opportunity to win a fight decisively and illustrate a fundamental learning point in terms of flow and decision making."
LCDR Michael Miller
F/A-18E Super Hornet pilot
U.S. Navy

MY NAME IS FLETCHER MCKENZIE, and I'd like to welcome to the sixth book in the *Lessons From The Sky* series. Before we take off, let me clarify the difference between TOPGUN and *Top Gun*...

They look and sound the same, but **TOPGUN** is the U.S. Navy school, and *Top Gun* is the movie. Other than having an U.S. Navy aviation theme, do they have anything in common? You're about to find out...

TOPGUN - A Navy Fighter Weapons School, established on 3 March 1969. A U.S. Navy institution that develops and provides graduate-level strike-fighter tactics training.

Top Gun - The first of two American romantic aviation-themed action films. *Top Gun* (1986) stars Tom Cruise, Kelly McGillis, Val Kilmer and Anthony Edwards. *Top Gun: Maverick* (2022) stars Tom Cruise, Jennifer Connelly, Val Kilmer and Miles Teller.

This book aims to share lessons from the U.S. Navy, inspired by TOPGUN - the air combat manoeuvring school. In the following pages, we seek to understand how the aviation industry learnt from these mistakes, so that others can learn and avoid the same errors.

As a child already interested in flying, and aiming to join the Royal New Zealand Air Force, I couldn't wait to see the movie *Top Gun* - the 1986 aviation-themed action film starring Tom Cruise, Kelly McGillis, Val Kilmer and Anthony Edwards.

I saw *Top Gun* in a small town theatre with my friends. With the perfect balance of action and good versus evil, it was released during the height of the Cold War, and featured the "best of the best" naval pilots training to be even better, climaxing with the U.S. Navy taking on intruding MiG-28s. Interesting fact — all postwar MiG aircraft in military service are odd-numbered, there-fore the MiG-28 is a fictional designation. To film *Top Gun*, F-5's were painted black with red stars. And although the movie never specifies the country of origin of the MiG-28s, the viewer assumes them to be from the Soviet Union or another Communist bloc state. The audio commentary on the film's "Special-Edition DVD" says that their intention was to imply that they were from North Korea.

As a moviegoer, *Top Gun* held me spellbound. Packed full of flying and action, I wanted to become an aviator. To help achieve my boyhood dream, I saved up to buy a pair of *Ray Ban* aviator sunglasses with mirrored lenses, and a white *Hanes* T-shirt, making me feel like I was halfway there. I never took up volleyball, but asked the hairdresser for a flattop haircut. Thanks "Iceman"...

As a child, I didn't see the movie depicting anything other than the good guys beating the bad guys (the Cold War narrative), with the bonus of the competitiveness between the pilots. Of *being the best*, I didn't consider the merits of aviation safety, or how "Maverick" broke the rules. The interesting fact is, as I became wiser around aircraft operations and cognisant of aviation safety, I realised it's all there, portrayed in the film.

Mike "Viper" Metcalf, the fictional commanding officer and instructor in *Top Gun*, points out that "Maverick" broke the rules bu performing a circus stunt fly-by, going on to say that the rules are there for everyone's safety, and that they not flexible.

Reflecting upon the movie, I recognise that the narrative contains an element of risk taking and of being an individual, versus understanding the overall teamwork, strategy, and the benefits of following operation procedure. There are infamous lines where "Maverick" misses the point, such as when Instructor Lieutenant Commander Rick "Jester" Heatherly extolls him never to leave his wingman.

The film, and its memorable lines of dialogue, increased the number of young men enlisting in the U.S. Navy, wanting to be naval aviators, by 500 per cent.

Over the years, I've used these lines in everyday conversation, along with the popular coughing "Bullshit" line . With that last comment aimed at Lieutenant Pete "Maverick" Mitchell after he and his Radar Intercept Officer (RIO) Lieutenant (Junior Grade) Nick "Goose" Bradshaw stationed aboard the USS Enterprise in the Indian Ocean, had just completed an interception in their F-14

Tomcat with two hostile MiG-28 aircraft (repainted F-5's from Miramar). "Maverick" escorts and saves his wingman, "Cougar" (and his RIO "Merlin") after being acquired with a missile lock on their aircraft–however he put himself and his own RIO lives at risk in doing so–all the while "Goose" keeps telling "Maverick" that they are low on fuel.

It's interesting to note that any trainee naval aviators caught repeating *Top Gun* movie quotes at TOPGUN receives a fine.

The draft *Top Gun* screenplay had "Cougar" crashing his F-14 while attempting to land on the aircraft carrier. His death was the original reason Maverick was "going to TOPGUN, in Cougar's spot". The U.S. Navy vetoed the idea, as they intended to use the movie as a recruitment tool, and didn't want any negative or a hazardous portrayal of serving on a carrier, or flying fighters.

Aviation Safety is very much a big important factor when operating machinery in the sky and naval aviation seems to have a few more risks involved.

The genesis of TOPGUN (not the movie) was in 1968, when the Chief of Naval Operations ordered Captain Frank Ault to research the failings of the U.S. air-to-air missiles used in combat in the skies over North Vietnam.

Ault concluded that the problem stemmed from inadequate aircrew training in air combat manoeuvring (ACM) and proposed to create an instrumented range to help aircrews become familiar with the complexities of firing their air-to-air missiles.

So, on 3 March 1969, the United States Navy Fighter Weapons School was established at Naval Air Station Miramar, California, on a shoe-string budget. And became unofficially known as TOPGUN. Eight F-4 Phantom II instructors from Fighter Squadron 121 (VF-121) "Pacemakers" and an intelligence officer chosen by a young naval aviator Lieutenant Commander Dan Pedersen. Initially based at Miramar, with the first headquarters being in a borrowed modular trailer unit.

It turns out that they were the "best of the best" and together, they revolutionised aerial warfare and redesigned the true art of ACM and fighter combat.

The overall objective was to build out, refine, and teach fleet air crews aerial dogfight tactics and techniques, based on the concept of dissimilar air combat training (DACT). They used spare aircraft (borrowed these aircraft from various Miramar-based units) to replicate enemy aircraft used by opposing global forces. Then the popular "opposing" aircraft were the Russian-built Mikoyan-Gurevich MiG-17, NATO code "Fresco", and the supersonic MiG-21, NATO code "Fishbed". TOPGUN teaches fighter and strike tactics and techniques to selected naval aviators and naval flight officers.

Research for this book uncovered interesting facts putting naval aviation operations, training and the *Top Gun* movie storyline into perspective.

Over the last 30 years, friends have asked, "Could the F-14 go into a flat spin and would you be able to eject safely?" From my small knowledge of jet flying, I used to say, "That's Hollywood, don't believe everything you see". But with the internet, we all have access to specialists, ex naval aviators, instructors, armchair experts and aviation themed blogs and forums from all over the world. The best way to fill more than a few hours.

One expert I found is Dr. Steven C. Schallhorn. Selected from hundreds of qualified naval officers to serve as combat instructor at the Navy Fighter Weapons School instructor (TOPGUN), Schallhorn taught air combat to fleet fighter pilots.

While at TOPGUN (the school), screenwriter Jack Epps, Jr. interviewed Schallhorn as he developed the script for the movie *Top Gun*. Some events in the film were based on Schallhorn's anecdotes. He explained how a flat spin could happen with an F-14 and that it, in fact, can complicate the ejection.

"The aerodynamics of the F-14 flat spin affect the timing of the ejection sequence. The canopy is jettisoned, followed by the ejection of the back seat, followed by the front seat. In a flat spin, the canopy, when it ejects, bobbles for an extra few hundredths of a second above the aircraft. That upset the engineered sequence because the guy in the back could then hit the canopy."

That sequence made it into the movie.

An article from 1977 comments that more recent mishaps indicate that the aircraft had a stabilised, disorienting, and disabling mode outside of controlled flight — the flat spin. I cover that article in the second lesson later in this book — "Tomcat Tailspin - Some Flat Facts".

The story states that the reason for the second F-14 Tomcat to go into a fully developed flat spin resulted from yaw generated by an extremis emergency during engine stall tests on a modification to the F-14A TF-30 engine. While conducting high-AOA (angle of attack) engine performance checks, the aircraft departed. As a result, one engine stalled while the other continued to provide CRT (combat-rated thrust).

As the pilot attempted to clear the stalled engine, the asymmetric thrust produced by the operating engine generated a yaw rate sufficient to cause the Tomcat to enter a flat spin. The pilot, though disoriented, was not totally incapacitated. Using lessons learned from the previous mishap, he requested that the NFO (Naval Flight Officer) eject while he remained with the aircraft in an attempt to recover prior to reaching 10,000 feet. Sadly, the NFO did not survive.

All those years and I had no idea how close to the truth the loss of Radar Intercept Officer (RIO) LTJG Nick "Goose" Bradshaw in *Top Gun* really was.

With an interest in aviation, and an evergreen love of the *Top Gun* movie, I have watched numerous documentaries, listened to countless podcasts, and have read a number of books and articles from various forums and blogs. Some resources worthy of a mention are:

Dan Pederson's book *TOPGUN - An American Story*. It tells the extraordinary, thrilling story of how the TOPGUN school saw the U.S. Navy reclaim the skies.

Pederson served during the Vietnam War, retiring as a captain, with 6,100 flight hours and 1,005 carrier landings and flew 39 types of aircraft. Quoted by CBN, "One of the great turnarounds in modern military history."

Another book I enjoyed was *TOPGUN Days* by Dave "Bio" Baranek, one of 451 young men to earn their Wings of Gold. He became the only one of that initial group to rise to become an instructor at TOPGUN.

In August 1985, Bio was assigned to participate in a Pentagon-blessed project to film the action footage for a Hollywood movie focusing on the lives of young fighter pilots... yep you guessed it: *Top Gun*.

In his book, "Bio" explains that they filmed many of the movie flying scenes from the specially equipped Learjet flown by the former fighter pilot Clay Lacy.

"I was to fly (aboard the F-5F) with Rat (Bob "Rat" Willard – the TOPGUN squadron's primary coordinator for the movie) who briefed the flight. [...]

We would have two F-14s and four F-5s available, but the first scene would involve only the two-seat F-5F flying in formation alongside the Learjet. On a call from the Lear, both "Rat" and I would look up, acting as startled as we could. Although there would be nothing above us, "Rat" explained how they'd use this shot - in the scene where "Maverick's" Tomcat is inverted above the MiG-28. The F-14 would be added later in one of the few special effects in the film."

He goes on to describe how hard it was to act "startled" in all his flight gear and oxygen mask. They don't train you for this at flight school!

In his other book, *Before TOPGUN Days*, "Bio" covers off the anxieties and excitement of entering the fast-paced world of flying jet fighters and reflects on what it took to become a TOPGUN instructor. He states:

> "Becoming the best doesn't happen overnight; you've got to work for it."

I reached out to "Bio" and he agreed to write the Introduction for the book. He generously allowed me to include one of his incredible and most exciting moments, titled, "Eject, Eject" — a heart-stopping lesson from the sky involving an ejection from a Tomcat in 1981 where the RIO survives.

Thanks "Bio". You can access "Bio's" treasure trove of incredible videos and other interesting facts and stories via his website: www.topgunbio.com

A good friend - Warner Cowin, an ex Royal New Zealand Air Force engineer (and pilot) and aviation enthusiast, asked if I had listened to the *Fighter Pilot Podcast*. If you haven't discovered it yet, then I recommend you subscribe to it as soon as you can. It is incredibly impressive. Hosted by Vincent Aiello, callsign "Jell-O", I asked Vincent if he would be interested in writing the foreword to the book. And he agreed. Thank you Vincent.

www.fighterpilotpodcast.com

The lessons and stories I have chosen for this book primarily feature aircraft from both the 1986 and 2022 released movies. If not the aircraft, then the pilot may be involved with TOPGUN.

The book breaks down the lessons into **before** the release of the 1986 movie, **after** the 1986 movie release, and then the 2022 movie aircraft.

With the release of *Top Gun: Maverick*, Tom Cruise returns

as Captain Pete "Maverick" Mitchell, a test pilot and flight instructor. The F-14 appears, with the focus on the Boeing F-18 Super Hornets. I've included a good number of Super Hornet lessons, which you should enjoy.

The American aviation classic, the P-51D Mustang, takes its place amongst the latest U.S. Navy fast jets, and stars as "Maverick's" own personal aircraft. It is in fact Tom Cruise's own P-51. The "Kiss Me, Kate" nose art was removed for filming. In the film, when "Maverick" is not educating the latest TOPGUN recruits, he is found flying high above the desert, enjoying flying the WWII flying machine. As a result, I've included some interesting stories about the P-51. Fascinating lessons from a very rare and expensive aircraft.

After 35 years of flying in the U.S. Navy, it's interesting to see "Maverick" is once again piloting an expensive experimental aircraft, type unknown. I cheekily assume that he may also have become the first (fictional) person to fly the next-generation hypersonic Lockheed Martin SR-72 Darkstar, apparently capable of a speed of Mach 6. Sadly no extra lessons for this very interesting Skunk Works designed ramjet aircraft! "Maverick" again risks his life, to get to Mach 10. I thought he would have finally learnt his lesson after breakingU.S. Navy procedures so many times previously...

Every day there are hazards and they are very real. Accidents and mistakes cost time and resources. They take the trained sailors, marines, and civilian employees away from their units and workplaces and put them in hospitals, wheelchairs and six feet under. Mistakes ruin equipment and weapons. Mistakes diminish readiness.

The U.S. Navy believes there is only one way to do any task: one that follows the rules and takes precautions against hazards. Combat is hazardous; the time to learn to do a job right is before combat starts.

This brings me to NATOPS. You will read this time and time again in the following lessons: Follow procedure.

The Naval Air Training and Operating Procedures Standardisation (NATOPS) program (pronounced NAY-Tops) prescribes general flight and operating instructions and procedures applicable to operating all U.S. naval aircraft and related activities. NATOPS is based on professional knowledge and experience, providing the basis for development of an efficient and sound operational procedure.

How do we know that NATOPS and following knowledge, experience and learning from lessons works? As Dave "Bio" referred to in his introduction, look at the U.S. Navy's data. In 1950, the U.S. Navy and U.S. Marine Corps destroyed 776 aircraft (roughly two aircraft per day or a rate of 54 major mishaps per 10,000 flight hours). From this, they implemented several initiatives, the angled flight deck on aircraft carriers in 1954, and implemented various standardisation programmes and procedures over the years. These changes were significant.

By 1961, the rate was at 19 major mishaps per 10,000 flight hours. By 1970, the rate was at 9 major mishaps per 10,000 flight hours, and by 1987, it was 2.7. In 1996, it was under two (1.84) major mishaps per 10,000 flight hours (only 39 aircraft destroyed). In 2020, it was down to 4 per 100,000 flight hours for major mishaps (Class A Aviation Mishaps (Manned)) — therefore that result is: by 2020 it was 0.4 major mishaps per 10,000 flight hours, demonstrating the key benefit of following procedure.

I am often asked what is the biggest lesson you have got from reading so many lessons and stories from pilots around the world?

My answer?

The consistency of following the correct procedures and not being complacent. Which includes the normalisation of operations that are not outside the airplane flight manual (AFM) or Pilot's Operating Handbook (POH) civilian speak for NATOPS. This helps mitigate the holes in the cheese lining up, i.e., the Swiss Cheese Model of Accident Causation (James Reason-1990).

An organisation's or pilot's defences against failure are modelled as a series of barriers, represented as slices of cheese, stacked side by side, in which the risk of a threat becoming a reality is mitigated by the differing layers and types of defences which are *layered* behind each other. The holes in the slices represent weaknesses in individual parts of the system and are continually varying in size and position across the slices.

The system produces failures when a hole in each slice aligns, permitting (in Reason's words) a trajectory of accident opportunity, so that a hazard passes through holes in all the slices, leading to a failure or accident. Therefore, in theory, lapses and weaknesses in one defence do not allow a risk to materialise, since other defences also exist to prevent a single point of failure. The model was originally formalised by Dante Orlandella and James T. Reason of the University of Manchester [1] and has gained widespread acceptance.

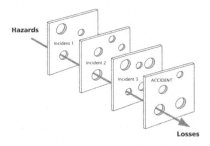

Adapted from the Swiss cheese model of accident causation. Created: 18 March 2014 Creative Commons - Davidmack

The U.S. Navy training systems, combined with NATOPS, ensures there are enough defences to eliminate the holes in the (cheese) layers lining up—even with more challenges in the sea environment.

We all learn from our mistakes. We can all reflect on experiences and situations and put the lessons into a format we can all follow.

I hope you enjoy the sixth book in the *Lessons From The Sky* series. Stay safe. Blue skies.

Fletcher McKenzie

HOW TO USE THIS BOOK

Each lesson has been replicated in the pilot's or crew member's words, without any editing other than minor grammatical corrections. You may notice some errors. We have purposely not amended the original reports.

A glossary of terms is included at the end of this book for your reference. Please note that this book may contain a mixture of both American English and British English, depending on who is telling the story.

If you find a term or an acronym in this book which isn't in the glossary, please email Fletcher:

fletch@avgasgroup.com

Each lesson has space for you to make your own notes if you want to. I recommend doing this to cement the learning.

Writing a short review of this book on your favourite digital platform, or on your personal blog or Facebook page, will help spread the word about aviation safety. Saving lives is the primary goal of this book.

THE NAVAL SAFETY CENTRE

The Naval Safety Centre
(NAVSAFECEN)

A continuously improving command that develops leading indicators of risks and hazards to empower all Sailors, Marines, civilians and their families to embrace a proactive culture of risk identification and management to achieve zero preventable mishaps.

The Naval Safety Center was established in 1951 at the Naval Air Station, Norfolk, Virginia, it was called the U.S. Naval Aviation Safety Activity. The staff collected, evaluated and published information about aviation safety. The staff also advised the Chief of Naval Operations and the Commandant of the Marine Corps on all phases of the aviation-safety effort.

Today, the Naval Safety Center is organized into four directorates: aviation, afloat, shore, and operational risk management/expeditionary warfare. Six departments and five special staff divisions provide support to the core operations of the command.

The Naval School of Aviation Safety in Pensacola, Florida, is also a NAVSAFECEN detachment consisting of civilian and military staff, which includes Marine Corps personnel. As an Echelon II command, NAVSAFECEN provides oversight of its single Echelon III command, the Naval Safety and Environmental Training Center in Norfolk, Virginia.

To preserve war fighting capability and combat lethality by identifying hazards and reducing risk to people and resources.

AVIATION SAFETY REPORTING SYSTEM

Aviation Safety Reporting System
(ASRS)

ASRS collects voluntarily submitted aviation safety incident/situation reports from pilots, controllers, and others. It then analyses, and responds to the voluntarily submitted aviation safety incident reports in order to lessen the likelihood of aviation accidents.

ASRS acts on the information these reports contain. It identifies system deficiencies, and issues alerting messages to persons in a position to correct them. It educates through its newsletter CALLBACK, its journal ASRS Directline and through its research studies. Its database is a public repository which serves the FAA and NASA's needs and those of other organisations world-wide which are engaged in the research and the promotion of safe flight.

ASRS data is used to identify deficiencies and discrepancies in the National Aviation System (NAS) so that these can be remedied by appropriate authorities. The data supports policy formulation and planning for, and improvements to, the NAS and strengthens the foundation of aviation human factors safety research.

CHAPTER 1

BEFORE TOP GUN

Lessons from TOPGUN *Aircraft and Pilots*
prior to the release of the movie, Top Gun

"Never stop learning. Those that stop learning, fail. School house training is the tip of the iceberg. Real training happens on the flight line, flight deck and in the work center. Leaders must encourage, prioritize and build training into planning."

CDR Tom Gibbons
Naval Safety Center
U.S. Navy

FEATURED AIRCRAFT

The following stories and lessons are from the actual aircraft, or variations of the these aircraft, featured in the 1986 Paramount movie, *Top Gun*.

Grumman F-14 Tomcat

The F-14 served as the U.S. Navy's primary maritime air superiority fighter, fleet defense interceptor, and tactical aerial reconnaissance platform into the 2000s.

The Navy made several aircraft from F-14 fighter squadron VF-51 "Screaming Eagles" available for the *Top Gun* film.

Paramount, the film studio, paid as much as US$7,800 per hour for fuel and other operating costs whenever aircraft were flown outside their normal duties.

Shots of the aircraft carrier sequences were filmed aboard the USS Enterprise, showing aircraft from F-14 squadrons VF-114 "Aardvarks" and VF-213 "Black Lions".

Douglas A-4 Skyhawk

A single-seat subsonic carrier-capable light attack aircraft developed for the United States Navy and United States Marine Corps in the early 1950s.

With the establishment of the Navy Fighter Weapons School (TOPGUN) in 1969, the availability of A-4 Skyhawks in both the Instrument RAGs and Composite Squadrons at the master jet bases presented a ready resource of the nimble Skyhawks that had become the TOPGUN preferred surrogate for the MiG-17.

TOPGUN introduced the notion of dissimilar air combat training (DACT) using modified A-4E/Fs. The A-4 was augmented by the F-5E, F-21 (Kfir), F-16, and F/A-18 in the adversary role, the A-4 remained a viable threat surrogate until it was retired by VF-43 in 1993.

Northrop F-5E Tiger

Replacing the successful F-5A, the F-5E and F-5F Tiger II were faster and have improved manoeuvrability. Already a small, highly aerodynamic fighter, it featured the newer compact but with high-thrust, General Electric J85-21 engines. The aircraft was a top performer with low cost maintenance.

The aircraft used for the fictional MiG-28s are Northrop F-5E (single seat) and F (two seat) Tiger IIs, which were used by TOPGUN as aggressor aircraft.

Following the *Top Gun* movie, some of the F-5s used as the "MiG-28s" maintained their black paint schemes and served as "aggressor" aircraft simulating enemy planes in the real life TOPGUN program.

Sikorsky SH-3 Sea King

Sikorsky SH-3 Sea King (S-61) is an American twin-engined anti-submarine warfare (ASW) helicopter. The Sea King performed various roles and missions such as, search-and-rescue, transport, anti-shipping, medevac, plane guard, and airborne early warning operations.

Aircraft carriers would typically deploy Sea Kings to operate near the carrier as a plane guard, ready to rescue air crew who crashed during takeoff or landing.

In *Top Gun*, Maverick and Goose are picked up in a Coast Guard Sea King. At the end of the film, after Hollywood and Wolfman are shot down, they safely eject and are rescued by a SH-3 Sea King plane guard.

In this book we have "Bio's" real story "Eject, Eject", which details how he and Switzer were recovered by the SH-3 Sea King.

EAST COAST ADVERSARIES

A-4 SKYHAWK & F-5 TIGER, FIGHTER SQUADRON FORTY THREE (VF-43) - CHALLENGERS

Richard P. Shipman, August 1977

"Ripper 2 from 1, the bogey's 280 at 5 miles, 15,000, he'll be coming down my port side."

"Ripper 2, Roger."

"Ripper 1, tallyho at my 11 o'clock, level. Migs! Migs! He's passing down my port side now!"

"Ripper 2, Rog, tally-ho. I'll stay high."

"Roger, I'm engaged. OK, I'm extending east. Can you get in for the shot?"

"Roger, I'm free. I'll be in for the shot in 10 seconds.
Tally and a visual."

"Roger 2, tally, no visual. . . Switch! Switch!"

"Roger, switch. Tally, visual. Pitch back starboard. I'm crossing your six. Check your 4 o'clock level."

"Roger, visual, tally. Unload to the south if you can."

"Roger, I'll take him southwest."

"Roger, don't arc. I'm in for the shot . . . good tone . . . Fox 21! Knock it off."

This dialogue is not an excerpt from tapes of a MIG kill during the Vietnam War, but it could have been. The engagement was, in fact, one of many realistic ACM training flights flown every day off the coast of Virginia and North Carolina to hone the skills of east coast fighter crews to a combat edge. VF-43, flying A-4s, T-38s, and F-5s, provides the "adversary" aircraft and pilots to accomplish this important training.

Early experience in the Vietnam War proved the necessity of maintaining basic ACM skills. To improve Navy aircrew efficiency in this area, an elite adversary training squadron, TOPGUN, was formed at NAS Miramar. The improved kill ratio of Navy pilots following establishment of TOPGUN proved the validity and effectiveness of an adversary program. But because TOPGUN does not offer day to day recurrent training for entire Squadrons and is located on the west coast, the need for an east coast adversary squadron became apparent. VF-43 was available and willing.

The VF-43 adversary role began by teaching defensive combat manoeuvring to A-7/A-6 pilots. VF-43 was – and still is – an instrument training squadron for initial and recurrent instrument qualification. The adversary program was established as a collateral function. Today, the increased emphasis on the adversary mission has resulted in specialization of mission for the ACM instructors (except CO and XO).

Realistic squadron training is the name of the game for VF-43 adversaries. Unlike TOPGUN, which trains one or two crews from a squadron who then return to pass their knowledge on to their squadron, the VF-43 concept involves entire squadrons. The basic syllabus is 3 weeks long, encompassing theory and practice of ACM, involving various aircraft numbers and types. Included in the training are 18 hours of ground school. Ideally, every squadron in an air wing would undergo the adversary training course once during its turnaround cycle.

"Instruction, learning, and ACM exposure in a safe environment is what we're all about," says LCDR Charlie Brun, VF-43 Operations

Officer. "Our syllabus is structured in a 'building block' style, starting out with basic theory and manoeuvres and progressing to 1 versus many exercises and squadron COMPEX (competitive exercise) if so desired. The beauty of our syllabus is that everyone in the squadron goes through it. We can structure our training for each individual's experience and ability level."

An important aspect of the training program is the ACMR (air combat manoeuvring range). This range has extensive and sophisticated equipment that records all flight parameters and aircraft manoeuvres during an engagement. This is extremely valuable for post-flight analysis and debriefs. The range is located off the coast of North Carolina and is the second of its type in existence. The first is located in Yuma, AZ, and was described in the MAY '75 APPROACH. Between the range and cassette tape recordings of voice calls during the encounters, the debriefs of aerial engagements have come a long way from the waving hands and loud voices of past years.

To accomplish its adversary mission, VF-43 has several types of aircraft. To simulate a small, manoeuvrable subsonic fighter, the A-4 (E or F) is used. The A-4 was originally the only adversary aircraft available, but it failed to duplicate the performance of later model foreign aircraft equipped with afterburners and capable of supersonic speed. Thus the T-38 and later the F-5 were added to the adversary inventory.

The T-38 is used as an adversary instructor trainer and for occasional engagements, but the squadron's F-5s are the heart of the inventory. Small, manoeuvrable, powerful, and difficult to see, the Tiger is an ideal adversary aircraft to simulate late model foreign fighters. It is equipped with manoeuvring flaps and has more thrust and fuel reserve than the T-38. It can also be equipped with the pods necessary to tie in with the ACMR. The squadron is presently borrowing the T-38s from the Air Force and hopes to exchange them for two-seat versions of the F-5 in upcoming years.

Squadron pilots were asked how the F-5 performed against the F-4s and F-14s it encounters in the adversary program. "Very well," commented LT Dan Gabriel. "Its small size and the camouflage paint job make it a real bear to see, and if you can't see your opponent, you're not gonna beat him. Learning to pick up a hard-to-see, fast moving opponent is excellent training for the type of situations the fighter pilot is most likely to encounter in any future wars."

Several of the instructors were asked to comment on the capabilities of the Navy's new F-14 compared with the older F-4. "There's really no comparison" says LT Mike Curtin. "The F-4 is pretty much limited to the vertical, so if you can get him into a turning fight, he's yours. The F-14, however, has the power to go vertical and can turn with you by sweeping those wings. It's really a tough fighter."

Since there are only a limited number of T-38s and F-5s in the Navy's inventory, establishment of supply lines and maintenance capability would not be efficient. Thus a core of about 30 civilian technicians from Northrop Aircraft maintain the eight T-38s and F-5s assigned to VF-43. Although this is an unusual situation, it has worked extremely well. The aircraft enjoy high availability (about 90 percent), a tribute to the experience and efficiency of the civilian workers. Undoubtedly a factor in the success of this concept has been VF-43's acceptance and integration of the civilians into the squadron.

As important as the aircraft are, the adversary pilots are the key to the effectiveness of the training program. Contrary to what some people might believe, the pilots of the adversary aircraft have to do much more than just mix it up and get to their opponent's six. LT Rick Owens, one of the experienced instructors, sums it up. "The instructors assigned here have to be outstanding pilots, of course, but they also have to know how to instruct. We have to make mistakes intentionally once in a while to get across 4 training point. We have to know how to set up engagements for maximum learning. We have to know how to brief and debrief the engagements. And one of our biggest responsibilities is safety of the flight."

Pilots selected for VF-43 adversaries are carefully screened for airmanship, officer qualities, and instructional ability. The squadron is looking for lieutenants coming off their first sea duty tour, with F-14-experienced pilots particularly in demand just now. Once the pilots have orders to the squadron, they go through an extensive IUT syllabus before they assume instructional duties. The typical sequence starts out with familiarization in the TA-4, followed by T-38 transition, A-4E/F checkout, and finally, F-5 qualification. Four different syllabi exist, one for each phase, and the phases are completed in entirety before the instructor moves on to another phase. The entire IUT (instructors under training) syllabus encompasses about 48 hours of flight time plus ground school. Aircraft systems training is accomplished to the A-4 at various training command bases, while a series of videotapes is used for the T-38 and F-5. The end result is a fully qualified instructor.

To the casual observer, dissimilar ACM between high performance aircraft operating at the limits of their envelopes might appear unusually hazardous. The excellent safety record VF-43 has enjoyed demonstrates that dissimilar ACM is not inherently dangerous when the risks are identified and positively countered. The emphasis is on safety throughout the adversary syllabus.

Lessons Learned:

Some of the steps taken by the squadron to conduct their unique mission with a minimum of risk include:

- Intensive and extensive briefs and debriefs.
- Well-defined rules of engagement that are inviolate.
- Monitoring by the range officer at the ACMR console.
- Close control of the engagements by the instructors.

Although all these factors are important, none is more so than the rules of engagement. Briefed on every hop, the rules of engagement provide hard and fast laws that govern conduct of the flight. Minimum altitudes during engagements, weather minimums, cloud deck clearance, radio/ICS procedures and disengagement criteria are all specifically spelled out. These rules are hard and fast; violations are grounds for terminating the mission.

Although the instructor pilot has overall responsibility for safety of the flight, VF-43 emphasizes that collision avoidance is both aircraft's responsibility. For example, the up-sun aircraft – regardless of who is piloting it – has the responsibility for collision avoidance since the down-sun pilot is very likely to be blinded by the sun. Similarly, there is specific action required of each aircraft in various potentially dangerous situations. In a vertical closing situation, the nose-high aircraft goes high. In a horizontal closing situation, both aircraft give way to the right. With aircraft closing at 1,000 miles an hour or manoeuvring at their maximum angle-of-attack, there can be no time for hesitation or uncertainty about what action to take if a collision possibility appears.

All briefs are terminated by a thorough discussion of spin/departure procedures. Fighter pilots know all too well that if they are not intimately familiar with spin/departure procedures, they will have little chance to recover from the highly disorienting and often violent gyrations associated with a fully developed spin.

Interestingly, safety records invariably improve the more ACM training is conducted. As LCDR Bob Brich, former safety and ACM phase training officer puts it, "Continued exposure to the air combat manoeuvring environment is vital in promoting safe aggressiveness. Not only do fighter pilot skills increase as a result of intensive ACM exposure, but accident potential decreases as familiarity in operating at the aircraft's limit is gained. Realistic, intensive training in a controlled environment is the safest and most effective way to ensure combat readiness when it is needed."

NOTES:

TOMCAT TAILSPIN
F-14 TOMCAT, STRIKE FIGHTER SQUADRON FOURTEEN (VF-14) - TOPHATTERS

LCDR J. A. Campbell, October 1977

The Navy's newest fighter, the F-14A Tomcat, has emerged as the most versatile and agile weapons platform to date. With the capability to stand off and fire the Phoenix missile at long ranges, its potential for revolutionizing air combat is unlimited. Beyond that, the variable geometry wing and high lift/drag ratio (aided by the aerodynamic effect of a fuselage tunnel created by widely separated engine nacelles) make the Tomcat the premier fighter in classic dogfight terms. Handling characteristics are such that since introduction to the Fleet, the aircraft has gained a reputation for uncommon stability and forgiveness in the high angle-of-attack/slow airspeed regime associated with ACM (air combat manoeuvring).

Recent mishaps, however, indicate that the aircraft has a stabilized, disorienting, and disabling mode outside of controlled flight - the flat spin. The history of the aircraft development and eventual recognition of this out-of-control flight condition may give Tomcat pilots an awareness that will enable them to prevent flat spins. It may also provide all aviators reason to review some basic principles of aerodynamics and handling characteristics of their particular aircraft.

Initial research and development flight tests in the F-14A documented its exceptional stability at extremely high AOA (angle-of-attack). Films depicting pitch pulses to greater than 70 degrees AOA reveal no lateral instability. Aircraft response to lateral control inputs at high AOA (above 18 units) produces rolloff in the opposite direction, which is reduced in rate-of-roll by disabling the roll SAS (stability augmentation system). The most frequently reported departure from controlled flight is termed a "coupled roll," in which rolloff induced by lateral stick deflection and aggravated by roll SAS inputs causes the aircraft to roll about its longitudinal axis. However, this is not a true spin, as there is no yaw-generated autorotation.

When flown to near-vertical (80-90 degrees nose up), zero airspeed, the aircraft pitches forward of its own accord to an extremely nose-low attitude, and, with neutral (hands off) controls, regains airspeed and recovers to level flight with normal back-stick pressure. Readiness squadrons demonstrate and teach these unusual attitudes and recoveries as basic confidence manoeuvres before replacement pilots begin ACM training. The general philosophy has been, "This aircraft can't spin unless you force it and hold in pro-spin controls."

The majority of F-14A aircrews have, therefore, been lulled into a false sense of security, armed with the experience of few and the hopes of many that, at last, they are at the controls of the plumber-proof fighter. Although this attitude may reinforce aggressiveness in ACM and confidence in the man/machine concept, it leaves the aircrew unprepared when thrust into the reality of fully developed, highly disorienting, auto rotational departures from flight (i.e., a spin).

Each aircraft has its distinct stall/departure/spin characteristics, and all aircrews must continually be made aware of recognition and recovery techniques. Early in the operational life of the F-14, numerous random "uncharacteristic" departures from controlled flight were associated with coupled roll manoeuvres in which the aircraft sustained an upright post stall gyration rather than a true spin. Recovery procedures were developed and verified for this relatively mild departure, and aircrews considered the likelihood of disorientation or incapacitation as remote. However, the F-14 community has recently discovered that the Tomcat will spin, and in a most disorienting and disabling mode.

The dramatic film record and aircrew debrief of the first flat spin (during the sixth flight in a series of 10 stall/departure evaluation flights conducted at NATC Patuxent River) changed the atmosphere of relative complacency concerning Tomcat out-of-control flight. A trained, experienced spin test pilot was nearly totally incapacitated as the result of approximately seven "eyeballout" longitudinal Gs. This jolted Fleet and Readiness squadron pilots to attention. The lack of immediate response to anti-spin controls drew concern. Spin tunnel and radio-controlled model tests as well as empirical data generated from the loss of the aircraft precipitated a rapid action NATOPS change that describes in detail the severity and complexity of the flat spin mode. Revised recovery techniques were developed to counter the spin.

Yet most aircrews believed that since the aircraft was deliberately flown beyond the onset of stall and aggravated by control inputs during the flight evaluation leading up to the departure/spin, that under normal flight conditions, entry into the flat spin was highly unlikely. A further restriction to disable ARI (aileron rudder interconnect) in aircraft so configured to prevent inadvertent pro-spin rudder inputs made the possibility seem even more remote.

Another reason for the theory that the Tomcat was immune to spinning was that pilots are extremely uncomfortable with excessive yaw rates. Therefore (it has been stated), they will not continue flight in a regime where yaw rate becomes so great that the aircraft (Tomcat) departs from controlled flight. The next two F-14 flat spins amply demonstrated that this seat-of-the-pants statement is unfounded in the dynamic environment of ACM or under the duress of an extremis inflight emergency.

The second fully developed flat spin resulted from yaw generated by an extremis emergency during engine stall tests on a modification to the F-14A TF-30 engine. While conducting high-AOA engine performance checks, the aircraft departed. As a result, one engine stalled while the other continued to provide CRT (combat-rated thrust). As the pilot attempted to clear the stalled engine, the asymmetric thrust produced by the operating engine generated a yaw rate sufficient to cause the Tomcat to rapidly enter a flat spin. The pilot, though disoriented, was not totally incapacitated. Using lessons learned from the previous mishap, he requested that the NFO (Naval Flight Officer) eject while he remained with the aircraft in an attempt to recover prior to reaching 10,000 feet.

After the canopy and rear seat (with occupant) separated from the aircraft, the spin increased in intensity, and the pilot realized he had lost control completely. The spin became more violent, pinning the struggling aviator against the instrument panel. Only with desperate persistence was he able to initiate ejection. Overshadowing the loss of the aircraft was the tragic loss of the NFO due to overexposure prior to rescue.

The third, most recent flat spin developed as the result of an abrupt, last-ditch manoeuvre to avoid an imminent midair collision. The rapid application of stick and rudder, aggravated by jet wash from the other aircraft resulted in an engine stall as the aircraft departed from controlled flight. The pilot attempted an air-start, but felt he had lost control of the aircraft. At 10,000 feet, the crew ejected with the aircraft in a flat spin to the left. Clearly, the pilot had to react to several immediate emergencies and was unable to analyze and correct for the onset of an unacceptably high yaw rate. The mishap occurred at medium altitude (approximately 12,500 feet), leaving little time for recovery once the aircraft entered a fully developed flat spin.

All three of the above aircraft entered the flat spin because of continued asymmetrical flight in a regime beyond published allowable sideslip limitations. Pilots were unaware of or unable to evaluate and counter the effect of excessive yaw rate, and the aircraft abruptly entered a deadly flat spin.

To date, three documented flat spins have cost the Navy one crew member and three aircraft. This distressing statistic applies to what is regarded as the most forgiving, stable aircraft in the inventory. Any F-14 aviator who has not yet recognized the potential for out-of-control flight in this aircraft is ignoring the recent events. Perhaps the old adage, "There are those who have, and those who will," applies. Evaluation of Tomcat flat spins led to a revitalized, detailed revision of NATOPS spin/departure recovery procedures. Emphasis on flight characteristics and aircraft limitations has provided a series of meaningful, well annotated procedures, which, coupled with flight simulator spin demonstrations, have more fully prepared Tomcat crews to cope with out-of-control flight.

The following lessons learned may help prevent future losses resulting from flat spins:

Lessons Learned:

It is essential that aircrews be briefed and prepared for out-of-control flight beyond the superficial limits of programmed recitation of recovery procedures. Recognition of stall/spin entry, intolerable yaw rates and tumbling, and disorienting flight prior to spin development, especially at lower altitudes, is mandatory. Past mishaps involved extremely high yaw rates, indicating that crews may be preoccupied by other emergencies and not able to counter the engine/control inputs that accelerate the stall and yaw rate beyond recovery. Pilots must be responsive to adverse yaw and neutralize controls early in a departure.

- The violence and disorientation of any out-of-control
  flight may stupefy or otherwise incapacitate the pilot.
  The aircrew must act as a team from the initial departure
  if they are to successfully recover the aircraft. In the F-14

flat spin, the pilot suffers the effects of two to three more eyeball-out longitudinal Gs than the NFO because of the front seat's increased distance from the spin axis. NFO verbal assistance can help orient the pilot, key him to note direction of the spin, and reinforce his application of recovery controls. Furthermore, in the event of loss of control below 10,000 feet AGL, the NFO can more easily jettison the canopy and initiate command ejection.

- The shoulder harness inertial reel is ineffective under 5-6 longitudinal Gs. Pilots must lock the harness at the onset of any violent departure from controlled flight before the effects of longitudinal Gs pin them to the instrument Panel, resulting in total incapacitation.
- Departures are aggravated by asymmetrical thrust and by engine stalls while operating in afterburner. Prolonged out-of-control flight with only one engine at MRT or CRT increases the probability of a runaway yaw rate.
- Consciously cross-controlling the aircraft in an effort to counter rolloff at high angles-of-attack flight may lead to snap departures and a flat spin.
- The recovery procedures for the Tomcat flat spin have been tested by spin tunnel and radio control model and will work. However, the control inputs are not dramatic, and a significant number of turns may be required to recover. Lateral stick (differential tail) is the most effective recovery control input. Insufficient altitude, as in the third mishap, leaves little time to let the recovery inputs take effect. However, with sufficient altitude, the aircraft exhibits indications that recovery controls are taking effect. The nose of the aircraft begins to oscillate from the horizontal, and as the aircraft descends to more dense air, the nose continues to remain below the horizon until the aircraft enters a more normal spiralling spin. If

aircrews recognize this reaction to controls well above 10,000 feet, they may anticipate recovery and have confidence in their procedures/control inputs.

The F-14A is designed to provide superior performance and manoeuvrability at the edge of the envelope. To knowingly exceed the design limits or experiment in regions of high angle-of-attack increases the possibility of out-of-control flight. All fighter/attack aircrews live with the reality of aerodynamic limitations.

The Tomcat exhibits no startling aerodynamic revelations and has proven worthy of the respect and awareness required of all previous tactical jet aircraft. The way to prevent future spin/departure aircraft losses is basic: know your limits, know aircraft operating limits, recognize loss of control, and effect the proper recovery procedures. With fully prepared aircrews conducting realistic training throughout the envelope of the aircraft, the Navy will continue to excel in ACM without the costly loss of aircraft and aircrews due to out-of-control mishaps.

NOTES:

EJECT! EJECT!

F-14 TOMCAT, FIGHTER SQUADRON TWENTY FOUR (VF-24) - FIGHTING RENEGADES

David "Bio" Baranek, December 1981

On 19 December 1981, the aircraft carrier USS Constellation (CV-64) was near the middle of the Indian Ocean on an extended deployment. I was an F-14 Tomcat Radar Intercept Officer (RIO), rank of lieutenant (junior grade), and had been in the squadron a little more than seven months.

My flight brief began at 1:15 PM and I was scheduled as a spare. We manned spares in case an aircraft broke during startup, so a replacement was ready to go. Just as the brief started, the pilot who was supposed to lead our flight launched as a spare for the event before us. Scheduling like this was a common gamble, and this time we lost. Another pilot was available to fill in, and I was his regular RIO, so I moved up from spare to flight lead. No big deal, last minute substitutions happened all the time.

It was a routine training flight, our Tomcats running radar intercepts against A-7 Corsair IIs. My pilot and I launched at 3 PM and expected to be back in time for dinner. It was another perfect tropical day with a few small clouds. Repetitious but remarkably beautiful.

Two hours after launch we were in low holding, watching the next event launch from the flight deck 2,000 feet below, with our squadron mate on our wing. As the last aircraft moved to the catapult, my pilot led our flight into the overhead break. On downwind we configured the jet for landing. I had 79 carrier landings under my belt and was pretty comfortable in the environment. I noticed the time was 5:15 PM as we made sighted the ball (the Optical Landing System) that would guide the pilot through the final approach. I thought about having a cheeseburger for dinner, and then we slammed onto the flight deck.

My next conscious thought, a fraction of a second later, was that something was wrong. I should have been thrown forward into my shoulder straps by the sudden deceleration of the trap, but after a brief jolt I was sitting upright.

I experienced time distortion, where each sliver of time contains many thoughts. Without consciously moving them, I realized that my hands were on the lower ejection handle on the front of my seat. I knew instinctively that if I pulled that handle there would be no turning back—our seats would rocket us out of the plane. I watched Constellation's island, the towering structure that holds the ship's bridge, sweep by as we rolled through the landing area past other aircraft. A second of silence passed over the ICS while both of us processed the situation.

As we rolled along the deck, some resistance slowed us down, but not enough to bring our jet to a stop. In a normal trap, the arresting wire plays out under tension and the rollout of several hundred feet of cable takes about two-seconds. For those seconds my brain was registering that there was still a chance we would come to a stop. We reached the end of the angle deck traveling about 50 knots - too fast to stop, too slow to fly.

Over the ICS my pilot called, "Eject! Eject!" His voice had an urgency – What are you waiting for? His hand was on the stick, still trying to fly, so it was my job to pull the handle that would eject both of us. I reacted on his first syllable, yanking the ejection handle. Everything that followed was automatic.

Explosive cord destroyed the latches securing the canopy to the aircraft and it flew free. My Martin-Baker GRU-7A ejection seat started running through its programming. Once the canopy cleared the aircraft, the rocket in my seat fired. I instantaneously experienced an acceleration force of about 20 g and blacked out for a few seconds.

My next conscious thought was profoundly confused: I wondered how old I was. But soon I remembered that I had ejected from an F-14, and suddenly I was back in real time. I could hear the wind and feel myself flying through the air.

People on the flight deck saw our jet disappear over the edge of the deck and then me, a second later, ride my seat to height of the tail-fins of planes on deck. This meant I started descending, unconscious and with an unopened parachute, from about sixteen feet above the steel surface. Fortunately our jet tilted to the left as it slipped over the edge, otherwise I would have free-fallen to the deck rather than splashing into the ocean.

Sensing a low-altitude ejection, the seat went through its sequence quickly. It severed the straps that held me in place, and I felt my parachute deploy and blossom. I felt a jerk as the nylon lines attaching me to the chute took tension. I opened my eyes just in time to splash into the water.

To prevent pilot-RIO collisions during ejection, the rocket in the pilot's seat fired four-tenths of a second after the RIO's. This meant that the pilot's seat launched an instant before our jet hit the water. The Tomcat had tilted more left-wing-down, so he was rocketed almost horizontally. The landing signal officers said he skipped several times across the surface of the ocean.

I splashed into the water and had been submerged for only a fraction of a second when the FLU-8P device was activated by salt water and inflated my life vest. I bobbed to the surface aware and alert. With my head above water, I unclipped my oxygen mask.

It was daytime. The water was warm, about 85 degrees. I had

landed just a few feet from the nose of my jet, which I was amazed to discover was also floating. The sight of the F-14, with the Constellation behind it, is one of the most memorable things I've ever seen. But I had things to do.

My first task was to detach myself from my parachute, because in training they'd taught us that a parachute doesn't float on the surface, but instead fills with water and sinks. I flung off my wet gloves with a flick of each wrist and released the fittings of my parachute harness, but discovered a new challenge: I was surrounded by my parachute and tangled in its tough nylon lines. Moving in the water only entangled me more. Not a problem, I had trained for this, too. Bobbing on the large swells spawned by the carrier, I calmly paddled backwards away from the chute. After only a few strokes, I could tell this procedure wasn't working like it had in the pool in Pensacola. I was only getting more tangled up. I was growing concerned about becoming trapped.

In a pocket on the right front of my survival-gear vest I had a razor-sharp folding knife, standard issue for cutting through parachute lines. But in training they warned us to cut lines only as a last resort. "Cut one line, and it becomes two lines." Backing out wasn't working so I decided to cut my way out. I retrieved the orange-handled knife.

I tried to use the curved safety blade, but it didn't work at all, so I went for the four-inch straight blade. There had been a problem with the blades opening inadvertently during equipment inspections, so the survival equipment riggers duct-taped the blades closed. Using my thumbnail I found the end of the tape and opened the blade, then scooped together a loop of parachute lines with my left hand and sliced through it with my right. The straight blade succeeded where the curved blade failed, and the lines cut away cleanly. I was frankly amazed at how well it worked.

Time in the water, less than a minute.

The rest of the event went smoothly. A big SH-3 Sea King helicopter, on "plane guard" duty, was over my head quickly, which was a great relief. They flew off to visually check on my pilot, and he saw me dealing with my parachute so he waved them back to me. Good thing.

The helo lowered a rescue sling on a cable and dragged it to me. I wrapped the sling around myself and they pulled me up. We then flew back to the pilot and a rescue swimmer was lowered into the water to assist with his rescue.

Back aboard the carrier the helo crew told us why the pilot got a swimmer and I didn't: they saw my parachute starting to be drawn into the ship's swirling wake and didn't want me to get dragged under, so they lowered the cable, which was quicker.

We also learned what happened to our arresting cable. The short story is that the crewman assigned to set the cable for the weight of each aircraft was untrained, and his supervisor was performing maintenance. There were backup gauges to show the cable setting, but the gauges for the cable we caught had been broken for some time. All necessary elements of the error chain were in place. We were all lucky there was no loss of life, only a Tomcat – and it could be replaced.

Lessons Learned:

The biggest lesson for me was the value of training. When I was in the water, the training I'd completed nearly 2 years prior came immediately to mind and helped me survive. In addition, aviators in my squadron had a habit of quizzing each other on the location of items in the survival vest, and when I needed my shroud line cutter, I knew instinctively where it was.

NOTES:

EJECTION OPTIONS

F-14 TOMCAT, F-8 CRUSADER, A-7E CORSAIR, CARRIER AIR WING SIX (CVW-6)

Commander, Capt. Edward K. Andrews, December 1983

After weeks of waiting and of warning the other side, and after an unexpected tune-up in Grenada, we'd mounted an alpha strike on the Shouf Mountains above Beirut.

Our F-14s had been fired on during several of their reconnaissance missions, and the U.S. finally committed some of its assembled carrier air power. We'd got planes from two carriers, Independence and Kennedy, in a combined strike against rebel positions in the mountains. The rebels were well supplied with Soviet shoulder-launched SA-7s. It wasn't going be a cakewalk.

I've been there before. In 19 years of flying, I've seen a bit of combat: Vietnam (downtown Hanoi is lovely when the SAMs light off), off the Israeli coast in 1967 and 1973, flying CAP during the Iranian hostage exchange, and playing tag with Khaddafi's fighters in 1981. Those MiG-25s are big slow-turning hogs, but boy do they move!

Yeah, I've seen a lot, but damn, I've never seen so many SAMs!

Look at them coming out of those hills! They're all headed for us! Everybody and his brother must have a "bottle rocket."

I just took a hit! I'm on fire! The airplane's not responding. I've got to get out now! No, wait — I'm still over the mountains. Who knows who's waiting down there for me if I punch out? If I can get the A-7 out over the water, I've got a better chance of being rescued by friendlies. OK, settle down and get the RAT deployed. The airplane's responding and I've got control again. At least I can direct it.

Eighteen years ago, I might not have made such a rational decision to stay with my airplane. Eighteen years ago, I didn't have much of a choice. I didn't have much experience either. I was an ensign with 25 hours in the F-8, still in the RAG. I was out on a night hop. The weather was pure dog. During the approach to Cecil, at 1,200 feet, I experienced an instantaneous engine seizure due to compressor failure. There was nothing I could do. I pulled the handle.

Ten years later, after a tour in Vietnam, I found myself flying F-14s.

We briefed for a one-on-one fight with the local aggressor Squadron. The hop went as planned, but on the return flight home, the cockpit lit up in front of me.

Circuit breakers started popping and fire lights were glowing. The cockpit rapidly filled with thick black smoke. My RIO didn't answer my calls. I couldn't see. There was an explosion, and I was bent forward in my seat.

Almost without thinking, I reached between my legs and pulled the secondary handle. Miraculously, the Smoke cleared, and I could see the instruments and then, *blam*. I was out!

The canopy had blown off, and the resulting rush of air had sucked the choking smoke from the cockpit immediately before the seat fired. My RIO didn't make it. The fire had eaten through some of the detonating lines leading to his seat, making the entire system inoperative.

In Vietnam, I'd once taken some damage in the afterburner due to concussion from an exploding SAM. I didn't think the F-8 was going to make it back, but it did. I had time to think about it, hanging 6,000 feet over North Vietnam.

But now, 4,500 feet above the Shouf Mountains in Lebanon, there's a silence where my engine should be. Obviously, I'm riding on borrowed time. If I can just get it out over the water.

Suddenly, the burning tail drops off, and the forward fuselage with me inside begins to tumble end-over-end. This is it! My options are gone.

I pull the curtain and shoot out of the Corsair, which turns back toward the town and unfortunately falls into an apartment house. I'm over land, but closer to the water than if I'd punched out right after being hit. The improved four-line release allows me to side-slip until I get off shore, where I make a safe water landing.

After three boat transfers, I am airlifted by a Lebanese Armed Forces helicopter to friendly headquarters. Four hours later, I'm back on the Independence.

Lessons Learned:

As long as there are alternative options, I've found it is best to use them. You have to think, sort out the options available and stick with your decisions.

If I had not been presented with an alternative or not elected to sort out my situation, I could have wound up another statistic. It happens during routine operational flights, as well as during combat. Premature action or reacting without thinking can hurt you in the crunch.

Captain E. K. "Hunyak" Andrews

Former director of aviation safety programs for the Naval Safety Center, and Commander, Air Wing 6. He participated in aerial strikes in Grenada and Lebanon in 1983.

NOTES:

FIGHTER READINESS

VARIOUS AIRCRAFT, COMMANDING OFFICER OF NAVY FIGHTER WEAPONS SCHOOL (TOPGUN), DEC. 1980 - JAN. 1982 - CAPTAIN ROY CASH

Lieutenant Commander Bob Frantz, February 1984

Captain Roy Cash has been able to make a contribution to maximum fighter readiness by teaching not only what he has learned through training but also by being in the heart of the fight during the Vietnam War when Navy fighter effectiveness zoomed from a 2.5-to-1 kill ratio early in the war to 13-to-1 by 1972.

On July 10, 1968, Lt. Cash with about 30 combat missions behind him and 500 hours in the F-4 (plus another 400 in the backseat), together with his RIO Lieutenant Junior Grade Ed Kain, became the first AirLant (Naval Air Force Atlantic) crew to down a MiG. Cash explains:

> "We were in a VF-33 section 15 to 20 miles east of Vinh, flying off America, when we received a hot vector from Horne [CT-30, then DLG-30].
>
> We had two MiG-21s in front of us at about 4,500 feet.

I fired the first Salvo of two Sparrows, which I learned later did little except to alert them to our presence. Almost simultaneously with an E-2 call, 'Heads up, two blue bandits west,' two more MiG-21s popped out of the weeds. They had been low enough to escape Horne's radar.

The fight lasted less than a minute and a half but, because of the anxiety and emotion of the moment, I will never forget any one of those 87 seconds. It was nothing like anything I've ever encountered in flying prior to it or since. Nothing could compare in intensity.

After a couple of turns and a roll outside, manoeuvred into position for a good Sidewinder shot. I saw their flight leader's aircraft explode and was rather relieved to see the pilot in a parachute. I didn't want to kill the guy. I felt I had accomplished my mission by rendering his machine impotent to fight again. The other three MiGs left the fight at that point."

It was later learned that the destroyed MiG-21 was flown by an NVAF (North Vietnamese Air Force) Lieutenant Colonel with several American kills. Cash was awarded the Silver Star for his success.

Capt. Cash feels that had the F-4 crews had the benefits of the training that today's crews receive, the engagement would have resulted in two, possibly three, MiG-21 kills.

"In 1968, there was still little air combat manoeuvring (ACM) training. The replacement air group (RAG) squadrons had no formalized syllabus, and TOPGUN was not yet established. ACM in the Phantom was in its embryonic stage. The thinking in the F-4 community had been that with the Phantom's head-on capability 'we'd shoot the bogey before he was ever aware of our presence.'

We trained more for the intercept than for the engagement. Vietnam taught us, because of the frequent need for visual identification, that it was often necessary to engage. That meant we had to know tactics and our weapons systems, as well as the tactics and weapons systems that would be employed against us. Had I been a lieutenant with to-day's training, I would not have fired the Sparrows when I did. I wasted two missiles. I would have known from my training to wait until I was more fully in the envelope before firing."

On a personal level, the veteran fighter pilot with more than 300 combat missions, 4,000 jet hours and 1,200 traps encourages crews "to get to know each other as well as possible. Train together, fly together, work together and play together. Know how each other thinks. The objective is to fight as one."

Cash calls the lieutenant fighter pilot or RIO "the best stage in life for anybody to be." He explains, "At that point, you're ambitious, highly motivated, and have lots of energy and drive. You have enough experience to prosecute the mission, but you're eager to learn and not so cocky from your acquired experience that you think you know it all. It's still early enough in your career that you can concentrate on flying without being saddled with the responsibilities of rank."

It is interesting to note that Cash, a 1962 Memphis State University graduate with an English and Theatre major, feels that technically educated people generally make the best fighter crew candidates. The fighter wing commander feels that, "Engineering, math, physics, computer science and related disciplines give you the edge."

"Fighter aviation is more than just flying. I could probably teach my mother to fly, but she wouldn't make a good fighter pilot. The best ACM driver isn't necessarily the best stick and throttle aviator. It's assumed he has excellent motor skills when he gets wings and certainly when he gets fighters.

Those who excel understand complex systems and how to employ those systems, and can effectively analyze dynamic relationships in the air."

He describes the wing's mission as training. "It is my job to ensure that our squadrons preparing for extended deployments have the opportunity to take advantage of the maximum amount and quality of training possible. That includes everything from instruments to field carrier landing practice (FCLP), low-level ops, ordnance delivery, electronic warfare (EW) and, of course, ACM. Facilities, scheduling and funding are not limited to operations at Oceana either. Frequently, squadrons or detachments are deployed to or from Key West, Roosevelt Roads, Fallon, Miramar and Nellis Air Force Base, as well as other USMC and USAF fighter bases in the United States."

Among the wealth of training opportunities the wing encourages its squadrons to take advantage of is the Fleet Fighter ACM Readiness Program (FFARP). Conducted by VF-43, FFARP is a 17-working-day air combat training period when the fleet squadron pits its F-14s against adversary F-5s, T-38s and A-4s. The program, begun at Oceana, is conducted for West Coast squadrons by VF-126 at Miramar.

A quarterly sea battle exercise, Seabat, coordinated by the Fitwing staff, is an intensive, four-day, joint service, war-at-sea, electronic warfare exercise which utilizes electronic countermeasures (ECM) aircraft, early warning aircraft and strategic bombers, as well as fighters. The Fitwing also coordinates scheduling for VC-12, a reserve composite squadron which uses its A-4s for adversary services to the wing's squadrons and other units. VC-12, like VF-43, provides F-14 crews an opportunity to train against a dissimilar bogey.

Squadrons are urged to send at least one crew to TOPGUN at NAS Miramar during each turnaround. In this graduate level program aimed at the top fighter crews in each fleet squadron, students not only learn weapons and tactics, but substantial emphasis is placed on briefing and teaching techniques as well. The program is designed so that these nucleus crews will return to their parent commands and train the remainder of their squadrons.

TOPGUN also deploys two detachments to Oceana, one for a one-week Fleet Air Superiority Training (FAST) course and the other for dissimilar adversary training, using their F-5s and A-4s. FAST is a non-flying, EW oriented, maritime, air superiority course which utilizes simulators extensively to accomplish its mission.

Additionally, Fighter Wing 1 coordinates and encourages Oceana F-14 squadrons to take advantage of ACM training on its nearby Tactical Aircrew Combat Training Systems (TACTS) range against USAF F-15s and F-16s; participate in orange air operations where squadrons and air wings go to war against each other; and, when at the peak of readiness, participate in joint service Red Flag combat scenario exercises at Nellis Air Force Base, Nevada.

Capt. Cash urges squadron commanders to utilize every training opportunity available. For example, he feels, "A squadron needs FFARP in the same way it needs field carrier landing practice or carrier qualification to promote mission effectiveness. FFARP is integral, not optional. Every time a plane launches, it must have some element of training — some training goals and objectives planned." The veteran combat pilot considers Red Flag as the premier exercise for testing combat readiness. He calls it "as close to combat as anything since combat, and the best training package in the world. It is very demanding and very unforgiving. It is combat without shooting and killing people, combat without the bottom line. Because of its demands, no squadron should go to Red Flag without an intensive ACM and low-level operations workup immediately beforehand. I would consider the fleet fighter ACM readiness program a prerequisite. This is just not the kind of thing you go to immediately upon returning from leave."

The wing commander views the use of simulators, as "absolutely required for today's training requirements and complex aircraft. The simulator allows you to make mistakes at minimal cost. Of course, simulators cannot duplicate real flight conditions, weapons expenditure, carrier landings, etc. It's simulation only."

Similar ACM, F-14 against F-14, where an aircraft has the same flight characteristics and potential, and the success variable becomes the skill of the crew, is an area that Cash feels must be managed judiciously. He advises, "Keep it from becoming man versus man or pride versus pride. Where possible, it should be limited to orientation and indoctrination. Use it to demonstrate the employment of tactics or to show a single facet as opposed to going out to kill the bogey. An engagement that degrades into a low energy, low airspeed, rolling or horizontal scissors does no one much good. It shouldn't be like Dodge City. The objective shouldn't be to see who can shoot whom but to show how it's done.

"In dissimilar ACM, as in the FFARP syllabus, where each aircraft has inherent strengths and weaknesses, the bogey should intentionally give something away early in the training — do something wrong to see if the fighters capitalize on it. As the training progresses, the bogey gives away less and less, and by the end of the syllabus the bogey should maximize his performance and capabilities."

Anyone who has spent any time around Navy fighter crews, particularly since the inception of TOPGUN, quickly realizes that call signs have on many occasions replaced names as the primary method of identifying people. Marty, Lenny and Dan have given way to Streak, Toado and Bad in the airplane, ready room and at the club. Capt. Cash, call sign Outlaw, has mixed feelings about their use. "They have tactical benefits during ACM. It is a lot easier to call 'Joe Dog check Six', than 'Falcon Two Zero Three dash One check Six.' The problem occurs when they lend too strong an identity and reputation to the individual. It is important to keep the who out of intensive ACM training. What is important is not who shot whom but what tactics are employed and what is learned."

Lessons Learned:

There is little sacrifice of aggressiveness and there are few artificial limitations for the sake of safety in Navy fighter training. The Fitwing commander explains:

> "We train to the limit of the aircrew and the vehicle. There is a natural margin or departure point. To go beyond that violates safety and puts the crew in an out-of-control mode. If not in control, the crew is vulnerable. Therefore, it is a common sense limitation.
>
> We don't train ACM below 5,000 feet because it leaves no margin for error. If you have a departure [from controlled flight] below 5,000, you have to give the airplane away. You've got to get out immediately. There's no time to effect a recovery. So, we make 5,000 feet the ground, and the survival instinct and discipline keep us above that simulated floor. Safety equals professionalism."

With over 3,500 hours, more than 1,000 of his 1,200 traps and all his combat missions in the F-4, Cash has a special place in his heart for the Phantom. He is quick to note that, "April 1, 1984, was the twentieth anniversary of my first hop in the F-4, and June 15 the twentieth anniversary of my first trap. As far as I'm concerned, only two aircraft fall into the category of the word 'venerable' — the DC-3 and the F-4. The DC-3 is still flying after more than 40 years, and F-4s are still being flown by more Free World fighter forces than any aircraft in the history of combat aviation."

This fighter pilot's feelings about his airplane are expressed in an Ernest Hemingway quote he keeps on his desk: "You love a lot of things if you live around them. But there isn't any woman and there isn't any horse, not any before nor after, that is as lovely as a great airplane. And men who love them are faithful to them even though they leave them for others. Man has one virginity to lose in fighters and, if it is a lovely airplane he loses it to, there is where his heart will forever be."

As long as Top Cats like Roy Cash are around, the Tigers in the fleet squadrons out on the line can rest assured that their needs and interests are being well represented by those who live and love the fighter business.

On June 15, 1984 — the twentieth anniversary of his first trap in an F-4 – Capt. Cash made his last trap in an F-4 Phantom of VF-171 which was disestablished on June 1, 1984.

<u>NOTES:</u>

EMERGENCIES IN COMBAT

TOPGUN GRADUATE, 27TH TACTICAL FIGHTER SQUADRON, LANGLEY AIR FORCE BASE

1st Lt. Vincent J. Constantino, December 1984

TOPGUN graduate talks about how Emergency Procedures (EPs) might be dealt with differently in a tactical (real combat) environment.

After sitting in a combat air patrol (CAP) for a full cycle each day for the last eight days without any action, you are understandably excited when your two-plane finally is committed by AWACS. Two contacts. You see their pincer and deploy your wingman to out-bracket them. The shots are called and, going pure-pursuit at 10 miles, you obtain a tally. Then at eight miles, a master caution light appears. A glance at the caution panel shows you have just had a major hydraulic failure. The two MiGs are closing fast. What would you do?

You say, "Well, first I'd call 'Knock it off,' then I'd start a climb . . ." Try again.

"Well, I'd pickle a Fox 1, get a tally-ho through the TD box, select full afterburner, hit the deck and blow through supersonic." Still not right.

Discussion of emergency procedures (EPs) usually assumes a benign environment, i.e., daytime, in the local area, CAVU. What if you are engaged with a Flogger over enemy territory or rolling out on final for a low angle pass? It could even be at night. "Knock it off and climb" doesn't hack it when you see the proverbial master caution light. But neither does going full burner and hitting the deck, necessarily. My point is that, as they unfold in combat, emergencies can demand different handling than they would on a peacetime training mission. Like anything else we do, some thought, discussion and good use of simulator time will prepare us for most situations.

Pilots with experience in combat tend to have very strong ideas about certain EPs, and some may even have had an engine fire or a hydraulic leak or two over Southeast Asia. If you know anyone like this, tap this insight, even if it means having to buy him a round or two at the club. Finally, I suggest incorporating these topics into flight briefings.

Lessons Learned:

I wish to emphasize at the outset that the suggestions and facts printed here are not prescriptions for action in peacetime. Nor should it be read as a cavalier interpretation of published emergency procedures. I simply acknowledge that priorities may be different in combat when you are about to be shot! Certainly, three basic steps still apply, with qualifications:

1. Maintain aircraft control. Of course. If you hit the mountains, that solves the enemy's problem.

2. Maintain situational awareness. It is important that you remain aware of what is going on around you. Try not to focus all your attention inside the cockpit. Is your machine flying normally? How are the other aircraft reacting? Do they

know that I'm hurt? Which way is home? Do I have tanker support?

3. Analyze the situation and take proper action. This is not so easy anymore. Your immediate task may be to defeat an air-to-air missile or jink from AAA. Can you judge the extent of your problem with one eye on the caution panel and the other on the MiG? You may be so caught up with the fight that your first indication of a problem is an abnormal response to a flight-control input or adverse yaw.

Here's where your judgment comes into play. You must answer this question: How much is my performance degraded and what systems are affected? The extent to which you will be able to answer that depends on your general knowledge and, just as importantly, your familiarity with past problems in the systems of your aircraft. Why may a single generator failure be serious? Because at times in the past, it has been followed by a fire. Your type aircraft will have its own peculiar problems. Learn about them by reading all the mishap and hazard reports that apply to your community.

So, what should your first action be in a combat situation? Disengage. How? Think of a few situations and you will come up with some possible actions. You will need to do one or more of the following: Shoot a missile or the gun, drop a bomb, jettison tanks and/or ordnance, light the burners, head for friendly territory. Read almost any account of an emergency in combat, and you will gather that heading for home was foremost in the minds of those afflicted . . . drop chaff and flares, take it up, take it down, head for the clouds, point toward a safe area, etc. If you are defensive or neutral, your DCM skills will be tested.

Decide if you can get out of the mess on your own. Call for help; re-establish mutual support. If your wingie is there, be directive. Otherwise, get on the horn and see if you can get someone else on the way. Mutual support becomes paramount when a flight member is having a problem. Try to envision fighting your way out with an engine fire - alone! It's not a very pleasant scenario.

OK, now you are free from the immediate threat with your wingman in a supporting formation. What next? Head for friendly territory. Read almost any account of an emergency in combat, and you will gather that heading for home (feet-wet in Southeast Asia) was foremost in the minds of the afflicted. The pain and loneliness of a POW camp was well-known by pilots, so the incentive was patently obvious.

Consider what battle damage might cause: flight control or structural anomalies, oil/fuel/hydraulic leaks, injury to the crew. In this case, you may have a limited amount of time in which the aircraft is flyable, so you must know which way to point.

Land as soon as practical. Yes, and maybe not from where you departed! In fact, how about that highway landing strip marked on your chart? Look closely at a map of Southeast Asia and you'll see a number of these.

Your ability to handle an emergency situation may be hampered by a number of other circumstances. You may not have free use of the radios; you may be alone ("My wingman split at the merge, and that's the last I saw of him."); you could be injured (some AAA are pretty accurate); you may be lost. Think about how these would complicate your plan for a safe recovery.

There are many emergencies which would create special problems in combat: hydraulic failure, engine failure, structural damage, fuel leak, oil leak, bleed air light, etc. Even items that are briefed daily become totally different beasts when placed in the context of battle. Try using "Landing Immediately After Takeoff" given a configuration of three bags, eight missiles, a low ceiling and a runway that has just been cratered, as the emergency of the day sometime. That's one sure way to liven up your next briefing!

NOTES:

WHAT PRICE GLORY?

F-14 TOMCAT, FIGHTER SQUADRON FIFTY ONE (VF-51) - SCREAMING EAGLES

Lt. Mike Manazir, August 1985

As the Tomcat passed the bow of the CV, climbing to 600 feet, the pilot anxiously checked his gauges, noticing a left low fuel light. The right side was indicating only slightly more than the left.

Continuing upwind, the pilot spotted two A-7s on downwind. The Tomcat would have to go three miles upwind for interval.

"103, Tower, what's your state?

"2.5 Boss. "

"Roger, priority downwind."

Whew! Thanks, Boss. OK, one more time . . . this one has got to be a rails pass . . . not much fuel to play . . . with landing checks complete . . . A-7 in the groove . . . OK, turn now . . .

"103, Paddles, fly a slightly high, coming down approach. "

"103, Roger". . .

There's the ball just a little high, got to work it down. . .

"Don't Climb!". . .

Ball's coming down ... power back on ... Trap! Taxi one wire, but we're aboard. Wow, look at that; both low fuel lights illuminated! That was too close.

The outcome could have been a lot worse than a taxi one wire. How many young, or not so young, aviators have lost an airplane due to fuel starvation? How many more said it would never happen to them? Before this incident, I was one who scoffed at the idea of running my airplane out of fuel due to my own negligence. I have a different opinion now. Let's look at the events that changed my mind. The weather was typical for winter time I.O. 2,000 scattered, visibility 10 miles, seas calm, light northeasterly winds. Eight hundred miles from the nearest divert, the carrier was working blue water operations.

Returning from another uneventful CAP mission, we requested a low pass by the ship. Low pass approved. Great! Beautiful day, crews manning up for the next launch, lots of people on the flight deck. Great opportunity to look S. H. around the ship and show everyone what fighter aviation is all about.

Reporting three miles astern, I rechecked my fuel state. The totalizer indicated 6.5 (6,500 pounds JP-5 (military jet fuel)). Max trap for our configuration was 4.5. Next launch was in 15 minutes with three airplanes, recovery to follow. That left approximately 25 minutes until a ready deck. Heck, it's a nice day. That's plenty of gas (or was it?).

The RIO and I estimated the fly-by would take 1,200 pounds of fuel; however, we failed to recall that our assumption of 2,000 pounds per minute fuel flow in zone 5 A/B was based on data collected at 20,000 feet. Our actual fuel consumption was much higher at sea level, aggravated by four Phoenix rails, external fuel tanks and a full weapons load-out.

Selecting Zone 3 A/B, we commenced the fly-by. Nearing the ship at .93 IMN, I selected Zone 5 A/B and streaked down the port side, transonic.

"Looking good, 103, nice vapes!"

"Thanks, Boss, returning to low holding."

Great fly-by! I'll bet they got a charge out of that one! Held it in burner a little long, though. What's the fuel now? Hmmmm, 4.0 and it's still 12 minutes until launch; at least 20 minutes until recovery. At max conserve, that leaves us with 2.6 at the ramp. Two point six equals 400 pounds until low fuel lights, 100 pounds above day emergency tank fuel and 2,500 pounds below squadron SOP fuel on deck! Rats! We may have gooned this one. Well, we'll make it. Zip-lip recovery – no one will be any the wiser.

Holding overhead, we "hawked" the deck. At launch time, one Tomcat launched. The second airplane taxied over the JBD (jet blast deflector), went into tension and promptly suspended. The pucker factor got a little more acute. Check the fuel state: 3.0. "Charlie fuel" for the Tomcat is 3.40 daytime. Now comes the decision. We know we're going to be below "emergency tank fuel" (2.5) in just minutes and the deck is not clear. I goofed, but we've got to fess up.

"Boss, 103, we're Charlie fuel."

"You're what?"

Sure didn't sound like the friendly voice who moments ago told us how great we looked. I'll bet the phones are ringing right now between the tower, bridge and the ready room. Finally, the deck was clear. We broke, rolled into the groove with 2.7 and promptly got a technique wave-off. Turning downwind, we made one more pass and trapped, landing with 2.1. We went from a comfortable fuel state to below what's allowed all by ourselves. Although we were safely on deck, we learned a few more important lessons about carrier aviation.

Lessons Learned:

Don't be lulled by calm, clear days around the boat. What is the norm day after day can change in a heartbeat. The deck can go foul when you least expect it. Calculate fuel requirements exactly, keeping in mind the parameters used to provide fuel consumption figures. Plan for unforeseen circumstances. Above all, when you put yourself in an extremis situation and it's your fault, don't hesitate to admit it. Better to absorb some flak and a couple of no-fly days than lose an aircraft, or worse, an aircrew.

Aggressiveness needs to be tempered with responsibility and accountability. As one sage aviator so aptly put it, "Ten thousands attaboys are wiped out by a single Delta Sierra."

Lt. Manazir

F-14 pilot with the Screaming Eagles of VF-51.

A U.S. Naval Academy graduate, he earned his wings in 1983 and has logged more than 500 F-14 hours. His first WESTPAC deployment was on USS Carl Vinson (CVN 70).

NOTES:

DECISION TO EJECT

TA-4 SKYHAWK & F-14 TOMCAT, FIGHTER SQUADRON TWENTY ONE (VF-21) - FREELANCERS

Lcdr. S.E. Collins, September 1985

I was only five or six hops away from completing the RAG and being assigned to my first fleet squadron. The day began with two lectures and one trainer in the morning. However, the afternoon was different. I was scheduled for a back-seat ride in the TA-4 during a syllabus tactics hop. It was the instructor's hope that we could learn a lot by watching an engagement from the bogie's point of view. Little did they know how much I would learn that day.

The hop was briefed in detail with all contingencies covered. I was given a refresher brief on the TA-4 seat and survival gear. The first engagement went as briefed, with me spending most of my time looking over my shoulder looking down the intakes of F-14s. Just prior to "knocking off" the first fight, we were in a slow-speed fight and our TA-4 had a mild slat departure. When we recovered, I cinched down my lap belts because I remember having the feeling of being well off the seat during the negative Gs.

On the second set up, we rechecked the lap belts once more. Approximately one minute into the fight, I remember looking over my shoulder and seeing an F-14 that was getting ready to "shoot" us. I called for a break turn to the right. We were at 22,000 feet and 325 knots. I felt the "G" increase as we broke to the right, then suddenly the airplane departed violently to the left. I had the sensation of tumbling end over end three to four times. I looked to the left and saw that the slat was out and called to the pilot, "It's a stuck slat." I looked to the right and noticed that the right slat was out as well. I then called, "It's not a stuck slat."

In a matter of moments, the TA-4 had entered an inverted, hesitant spin. Despite my tight lap belts, I was completely up off the seat and unable to read any of the aircraft instruments. My helmet repeatedly struck the canopy so hard that the plexiglass cracked in several places. The pilot hadn't said a word yet, and I wasn't sure what the aircraft was doing. It would hesitate for a fraction of a second upright, with the "G" unloading, then tuck violently inverted.

I finally saw the altimeter after six or seven revolutions. The hands were a blur but I saw them pass 14,000. It was at this time I made the decision to eject if the aircraft didn't recover after two more revolutions. At the completion of the second turn, I reached for the lower handle and tried to get myself in the best position I could. I closed my eyes and pulled the lower handle.

In less than a heartbeat, I was in the chute. My first sensation was how peaceful and quiet it was. I opened my eyes and looked around and saw briefing cards everywhere. I looked below and saw the TA-4 spinning as it entered the clouds. A little below and directly underneath me was the pilot, who appeared to be unconscious.

I couldn't believe I had survived the ejection, but I was sure I was going to die because my chute would collapse from being blocked by the pilot's parachute. I ended up running across the top of his canopy and getting clear. Then I inflated my LPA and deployed the seat pan. I looked down in wonder as the lower half of the seat pan with my "charms" continued on its merry way to the water. The raft had inflated but nothing was weighing it down with the seat pan gone. It flew up into my face, then behind my back, tangling itself around my legs.

Just as I settled back to enjoy my first and hopefully last parachute ride, an F-14 flew by. He was in obvious pursuit of an imaginary Japanese Zero that was attempting to strafe me in the chute. I'd heard of "train like you'll fight," but this was ridiculous! The F-14 made several pylon turns around my chute before I made it clear that I would prefer to die at the hands of the invisible Zero than be eaten by a Tomcat.

As I prepared for water entry, I tried untangling the raft from my legs and get in it before hitting the water. The idea initially seemed sound; however, on second thought, I realized the upper half of the seat pan was still attached to my posterior. Knowing the raft would be damaged on impact with the water, I decided on a normal water entry.

When my feet hit the water, I released the parachute. My heartbeat had slowed to 250 so I took off my helmet and relaxed a bit, thinking life wasn't so bad, and I'm happy to say the helicopter pickup went smoothly for both myself and the pilot.

Lessons Learned:

1. An inverted flight check prior to any manoeuvring flight is an excellent way to ensure lap belts and loose gear are Secure.
2. Only rely on the gear attached to your body. I wear the SV-2 survival vest with 5 pounds of extra gear.
3. You don't need to fly close to aircrew in chutes to let them know you are there. All you'll end up doing is soiling their flight suits.
4. Never believe it can't happen to you. I didn't and it did. Be prepared.

NOTES:

SPIN AVOIDANCE VS SPIN RECOVERY. MUTUALLY EXCLUSIVE ... OR SUPPORTIVE?

F-14 TOMCAT, FLEET SYSTEMS AT NAVAL AIR DEVELOPMENT CENTER

Cdr J.H. Rockwell III, December 1985

Cold, calculating and high-tech we may be as fighter pilots, but we're certainly not immune to an "emotional issue" with regard to how we squeeze the maximum from our aircraft. Such an issue centers on the infamous flat spin of the F-14. The Tomcat community is unique in Tacair since there is no NATOPS procedure for recovery from a spin. (*Only upright flat spins are considered in this article. The terms "flat spin" and "Spin" are used interchangeably.*)

Chapter 5 states unequivocally that a crew which finds itself in a confirmed flat spin, as evidenced by pegged AOA (angle of attack), increasing yaw rate and eyeballs-out G. must jettison the canopy and eject . . . regardless of altitude . . . regardless of pilot incapacitation (or lack thereof). . . regardless of whether one or both engine(s) is are functioning normally.

Why is this? Is it because the F-14 is not recoverable from a flat spin? Far from it. Highly reliable evidence indicates that properly applied anti-spin controls will recover the F-14 with an altitude loss comparable to that of other high performance aircraft. Furthermore, timely locking of the harness should positively prevent incapacitation from eyeballs-out G. The reason NATOPS mandates ejection rather than recovery is to protect the pilot from the debilitating effects of eyeballs-out G if he forgets to lock his harness. If this seems an overly cautious approach, those who are new to the community will 28 understand the motivation better if it is put in historical perspective.

During the F-14's fleet introduction at Miramar in the early 70s, it was perceived as a magic airplane. Tomcat pilots beat up on their F-4 and F-8 adversaries with monotonous regularity due to the plane's superb manoeuvrability, acceleration, field of view and fuel specs. It was comfortable, easy to fly and Grumman assured us it would not spin. The plane encouraged its handlers to be aggressive in air combat manoeuvring (ACM); it did not seem as anxious to, "bite you" as the F-8 did, and it was so much more nimble than the F-4 that the effect was not unlike going from a Mack truck to a sports car.

Our euphoria was shattered in 1976 and 1977 when two F-14s were lost in flat spin mishaps at Patuxent River. From 1978 to the present, 12 F-14s were lost in out-of-control-flight (OOCF) mishaps (up-and-away flight only; takeoff and landing mishaps are not included), of which eight are officially listed as having been caused by a flat spin. Only one of the 12 included loss of pilot and RIO, who for unknown reasons did not eject. All 22 crew members who ejected escaped serious injury.

Why this change from the "spin-proof" days of the early 70s? Several factors were at work: increased carriage of external stores: engines which often stalled singly rather than in pairs, thereby aggravating a departure; a high percentage of ACM compared to total hours flown; and in many cases, a brief but critical time delay by the pilot during departure from controlled flight. A major effort at increasing pilot awareness was initiated by NAI C. NAVAIR and the model manager. A series of briefings and NATOPS rewrites took place which were designed to equip pilots with the information necessary to deal with inadvertent departures, sudden engine stalls or both in combination (they are mutually inducing in some flight regimes). Much of the information contained in today's NATOPS was gleaned from extensive contractor Navy flight testing with F-14 No. 1X, which is equipped with spin chute and emergency backup hydraulic system. These tests, conducted in the early 80s involved numerous departures under several combinations of external stores, but there were no spins, either intentional or unintentional (the F-14 has never undergone intentional spin testing).

Two undisputed facts stand out among all the official and unofficial information which abounds regarding F-14 OOCH: (1) proper and timely pilot action during the departure will prevent spin entry, and (2) a pilot who gets into a flat spin without locking his harness could quickly become incapacitated by longitudinal ("eyeballs-out") G, to the point where he not only cannot recover the aircraft, but could be injured in an ejection. These facts are at the base of today's philosophical approach to F-14 OOCF, which holds that since spins are preventable, we will not let the plane get into one, but that a pilot who is in one has no business attempting to recover the aircraft he must abandon it immediately, while he is still able. This no-option spin procedure has been combined with a very comprehensive and effective spin-avoidance program. All F-14 RAG students receive departure, OOCF training in the T-2 combined with lectures and simulator flights designed to help them deal with departures so as to avoid the spin entirely. The results speak for themselves: far fewer aircraft are lost in OOCF now than a few years ago. Unfortunately, the success of the spin-avoidance emphasis may have induced complacency in the community. It is virtually impossible to generate official reconsideration of the current NATOPS mandated ejection in lieu of spin recovery procedures.

Aviation, like most human pursuits, is subject to cyclical phenomena. We could be on the "down cycle" of spins at present, with an increase waiting in the future. The introduction of the F-14D, with its potential for higher asymmetric thrust, could present unanticipated problems related to OOCF. Would it not be prudent to reevaluate our NATOPS procedures with a critical eye, ensuring that mandated steps and supporting write-ups reflect the most useful and up-to-date information which technology can provide?

The Naval Air Development Center at Warminster, Pa., is equipped with a device called the dynamic flight simulator (DFS), which was not available as an F-14 spin trainer or research vehicle until 1984. The DFS is a centrifuge, a 50 foot-long arm which rotates in a horizontal plane, equipped with a gondola at the end simulating an aircraft cockpit. Although currently configured as an F-14 front cockpit, the displays and controls can be changed to simulate other air vehicles if desired.

Pilots strap into and "fly" the DFS in full flight gear, exactly as they would the real aircraft, and are able to experience forces on the body virtually identical to those felt in flight.

DFS motion is controlled by a CYBER mainframe computer, which derives its inputs from the flight controls operated by the pilot. The effect of pulling G's is provided by centrifuge arm rotation, while G axis is determined by rotation of the gondola (cockpit) around two gimbal axes.

Although physical limitations of the DFS prevent it from simulating the pure negative G sensation of inverted flight, it is well suited for generating the longitudinal G characteristic of the F-14 flat spin. Software control laws currently used with the DFS are refined to the point where each motion of the gondola is analogous to real aircraft motion; the pilot can enter and recover from a spin using exactly the same controls he would use in the aircraft, while experiencing the same physical impairments, such as eyeballs-out G and spatial disorientation. Results are clear and consistent: the F-14 simulation is recoverable, every time, with reasonable altitude loss, even when yaw rate has reached 150 degrees per second.

The DFS was constructed as a research and development tool. It is ideal for studying the effects of varying flight control inputs and engine thrust and has also incorporated new cockpit displays for pilot evaluation. An automatic harness locking device (triggered by a 0.8 longitudinal G threshold) has also been installed, and pilots are unanimous in their enthusiasm for it. But the DFS usefulness as a training device could play an equally significant role in its future. Although the benefits may seem obvious, it bears repeating that pilots who have experienced an exact simulation of the OOCF characteristics of a given aircraft are more likely to deal with it correctly when the situation develops in the aircraft.

Lessons Learned:

To return to the question implied at the beginning of this article, is there a case for re-examining F-14 spin procedures based on information learned from the DFS? The answer is "no" if we assume one of two things, either (1) departure resistance training is so good that there will never be another F-14 spin, or (2) the chance of pilot incapacitation in a spin is simply too great a risk.

The answer is "yes" if BOTH of the following are true: (1) properly applied recovery controls provide a high likelihood of spin recovery, and (2) the potential adverse consequences of ejection (i.e., back injury, drowning, hypothermia, capture by the enemy, loss of aircraft, etc.) are serious enough that the aircraft should be recovered if this can be accomplished with reasonable effort.

Right now the F-14 is treated differently from other tactical aircraft, in that spin recovery is illegal. This is in spite of the fact that the aircraft is arguably no more difficult to recover than, say, an F-4, A-7, A-6, A-4 or F-5. Pilot incapacitation is a serious problem only if the harness has not been locked. This has been verified by pilots experienced in both DFS and actual flat spins.

We are far enough removed in time now from the unfortunate days of the late 70s and early 80s that we should be able to examine the issue logically, and with a minimum of emotion.

Consider the worst case scenario: a pilot who finds himself in a flat spin during combat, with 32-degree whitecaps beneath him and enemy forces close enough for capture (if he survives the ejection and the first 30 minutes in the water).

Have we really served him well if our final word on the subject is, "Once a flat spin is confirmed . . . jettison the canopy and eject?"

Cdr. Rockwell
Associate Director for Fleet Systems at Naval Air Development Center, Warminster, Pa. Previously, he was at NAVPRO. Grumman, Bethpage, L.I., N.Y., and the Naval Test Pilot School, Patuxent River. Md. He is a 1966 graduate of the U.S. Naval Academy.

NOTES:

CREW CONCEPT
F-14 TOMCAT, FIGHTER SQUADRON TWENTY ONE (VF 21) - FREELANCERS

Ltig. Tom Powell, March 1986

I was a nugget Tomcat RIO on my first WESTPAC cruise. The ship had just left the Philippine Islands en route to Gonzo Station. Heavy flight operations increased the tasking on all of us, and the flight schedule was changing hourly. My day consisted of a midmorning Alert 5, followed by a mid afternoon Prisly watch, followed immediately by a brief for a two-hour air intercept control (AIC) mission and a no-moon night recovery. Because a flap asymmetry emergency occurred while I was in Prisly as the squadron rep, I missed my AIC brief completely. No problem right? It's AIC.

Back in the ready room I was met by my pilot for the event. A schedule change had netted me a different pilot than the one I normally crew with. Handing me a brief card he said, "Let's walk. I've got it covered."

Following a normal launch and check-in with strike, we were directed, "Mission change. Switch button 10." After receiving a hot vector we rendezvoused on two TU-95 Bears. The excitement of Bear escort was a welcome change from AIC and as darkness approached, the Bears went on their way. Since neither of us were seasoned Bear interceptors, the excitement left us somewhat unprepared for what was about to happen.

After one quick turn in marshal we commenced our approach and called the ball with state 4.6. "Hook-skip bolter," the LSO said as we turned downwind. "No sweat, so we boltered," I thought to myself as we set up for our second approach. That approach went well but ended in another hook-skip bolter.

As we turned downwind a slight uneasiness started to grow as we began to wonder if there wasn't something wrong with our hook. The third approach commenced and I called the ball with state 3.0.

Normal touchdown in the wires occurred but something was wrong. I didn't feel power come on and I didn't feel the deceleration of catching a wire.

We continued down the deck and time expansion began. The aircraft came off the angle at around 100 knots. As I felt the settle and saw the deck rise to my right, I realized I was already gripping the ejection handle as the boss screamed "Power, Power, Power!" My mind was rapidly calculating how far it was to the water based on how much the deck was rising to the right of me. I was waiting for the, "I've got it" or "Eject" call. Nothing. I was pulling the handle if we got any lower or if I felt a wing dip either side.

Suddenly, I felt power finally come on and a 30-degree wings level nose-up pitch attitude established. Again if I felt a roll-off, I was pulling the handle. The burner lit the night as I saw us climb back up past the deck and to 2,000 feet. Still shaking, we joined the tanker.

With refuelling complete and a quick hook check from the tanker, we set up for our fourth approach. This time, fortunately, we trapped.

Reviewing the PLAT tape opened my eyes to just how bad this bolter was. The pilot, engrossed with getting aboard, went to full direct lift control and idle on touchdown. Military power was not applied until we were past the wires and heading off the angle. The aircraft settled to within 20 to 30 feet of the water before burners and attitude pulled us out. Everyone I talked to thought ejection was imminent and expected to see chutes.

In reviewing this incident we felt the pilot was in error for not applying military power on touchdown and not establishing the proper attitude going off the angle. The fact that he didn't say either "I've got it" or "Eject" kept me guessing as to what the actual aircraft status was.

My failure to ask him, "Have you got it?" did not help. No longer were we working as a crew and I was left with the decision to eject or not eject, based on my limited experience.

Believe me, as a first-tour RIO, I was not prepared to handle this situation. It was later pointed out to me that had I pulled the handle we would have given 30 million dollars of good Turkey to the fish, but no one who saw this bolter would fault that decision. However, had the airplane been bad, and had I delayed the ejection, then we could be visiting St. Peter right now. All because of a lack of communication between cockpits during an emergency situation.

Lessons Learned:

The lessons learned were many. The importance of briefing the "what ifs" and what each aircrew is expecting to hear from the other during extremis situations cannot be overemphasized. We failed to do this because of a lack of time. This becomes even more of a factor when flying with someone other than your normal crew.

<u>NOTES:</u>

CHAPTER 2

AFTER TOP GUN

Lessons from TOPGUN Aircraft and Pilots
after the release of the movie, Top Gun

"Almost without thinking, I reached between my legs and pulled the secondary handle. Miraculously, the Smoke cleared, and I could see the instruments and then, blam. I was out! The canopy had blown off, and the resulting rush of air had sucked the choking smoke from the cockpit immediately before the seat fired. My RIO didn't make it."

Capt. Edward K. Andrews
F-14 Tomcat Pilot
U.S. Navy

THE BEST OF THE BEST

SEA CONTROL SQUADRON THIRTY TWO (VS 32) - MAULERS

LCdr. Smith , September 1987

We can still enjoy his antics on the silver screen, chuckling that it just isn't that way in the real Navy.

All through the deployment we kept hearing about the film, but no one on board got to see it. It usually takes awhile for the big ones to get to the fleet. Surprisingly there were no VCR copies of the film on board, so we had to be content with watching CVIC TV's washed-out version of the *"Top Gun"* music video and with reading reviews in 2-week-old magazines. Some critics called it the best movie of 1986; some even called it "The Best of the Best."

Engines on the fly-off aircraft were still warm, and welcome-home kisses were still on our lips when we trooped off to see the film. It was good: good story, good flying and good press for naval aviation. Kelly McGillis was great. Tom Cruise was good, too. I know a lot of women who really believe he is the best of the best. But for seasoned carrier aviators, he falls far short of being the best. It was fun to see how Hollywood portrayed our profession to the public. It wasn't hard to spot the flaws: a superSonic fly-by of the carrier without permission from the boss; busting ROE when intercepting a MIG; aileron rolls off the cat on an alert launch.

We all know these things would buy our hero an express ticket to a FNAFB board, and he would quickly find himself behind a desk with a Skilcraft ball point under his trigger finger. We can still enjoy his antics on the silver screen, chuckling that it just isn't that way in the real Navy.

"*Top Gun*" should be rated by the Navy as "Restricted to Mature Naval Aviators" – those guys who are smart enough to see through "the best of the best" syndrome of the movie. It implies that you can get a reputation for being the best by doing something bizarre, illegal or non-standard.

Yet, we've all heard it from the day we arrived at Forrest Sherman Field you get your reputation from doing it by the one who unfailingly arrives at the 90 at 450 feet on donut airspeed. He's the guy who pushes out of marshal precisely at assigned EAT, keeping bullseye and ACLS needles centered all the way to roger ball. The best pilot maintains 3 to 5 knots closure speed on the tanker and plugs the first time, every time.

Funny thing, you really don't have to do crazy things to get a reputation for being the best. Read the books, make them part of the very blood that flows through your brain and fingers, and follow them as a preacher follows the Bible. Pretty soon you'll be seeing green dots lined up beside your name on the greenie board. The OPS officer will be tagging you when a critical mission scheduled.

You'll be flying that Intruder tucked under the Skipper's wing when the order comes for a strike on a terrorist stronghold. Your Tomcat will be the one vectored to the critical CAP station when the Hawkeye calls for an alert interceptor. You'll get the nod when the admiral calls for a Viking to jump a meddling submarine. You'll be in the right seat of the Angel when human life is at Stake. And you'll be the only guy in the whole air wing who will stand up at Foc'sle Follies when CAG announces the name of the wing's number one Tailhooker.

Lessons Learned:

When you step forward to accept your award, you won't have to say a thing to those assembled aviators. You didn't get there by some Hollywood Stunt; you earned your title by doing it right – by the book, every time you strapped on your machine. You'll know from the sound of their applause and from the respect in their eyes that they know who is "The Best of the Best."

Once airborne, situational awareness is the key. The duties of the pilots must be clearly defined.

LCdr. Smith
Safety Officer of the VS 32 Maulers based at NAS Cecil Field, Florida

NOTES:

MY NIGHT IN THE BARREL!
F-14A TOMCAT, FIGHTER SQUADRON ONE
(VF-1) - WOLFPACK

Lt. L.P. Molloy, January 1988

What is a nugget pilot's biggest fear about going on his first major deployment? Is it having all his evaluations kicked back? No, he knows how to handle the maintenance officer. Is it being chosen as squadron first lieutenant? Definitely a scary thought, but being a competitive fighter pilot, he looks forward to the challenge of winning the Golden Throne Award.

How about the possibility of entering a hostile multi bogie environment with SAMs and AAA? No way. Being young and somewhat naive, the thought of applying his training to the real-world threat and maybe earning a Silver Star excites him beyond belief. That leaves us with the idea of having to endure the dreaded night in the barrel. After one particular night, I realized I wouldn't wish that "barrel" on my worst enemy.

It was one of those scheduled "pinky" launches with a night EMCON (radio silence or Emissions Control) recovery from "USS Boat" 700 miles from "NAS Anywhere". As my RIO and I walked to the airplane, we noticed the deck pitching quite a bit, but that wasn't unusual. We had been working MOVLAS (Manually Operated Visual Landing Aid System) because of pitching decks, for well over a week.

As we completed our uneventful CAP mission, we returned to marshal and pushed on our pre-briefed time. At three quarters of a mile, I looked out toward the lens and was overwhelmed. Although the ball was centered, the deck looked like a windshield-wiper going vertical (38 feet to be exact). "I've never seen this before," I thought. "Even though I'm single, my RIO is married, so maybe I'll add just a little extra power to keep us off the ramp."

As we crossed the ramp, the deck went down and we had bolter No. 1 (an aircraft fails to catch an arrestor cable). Being the second airplane to push from marshal, our downwind was extended to 10 miles before CATCC could hook us in. Approaching the ball call this time, I was determined to not only avoid fixating on the deck, but to concentrate on what the LSOs were showing me as well. Unfortunately, although I got a good start, the deck was foul and we were waved off for pass No. 2. Passes 3 and 4 were similar to the first one with the deck being out of cycle, resulting in bolters. Our fuel state was now down to 3.2, and our signal was "tank." The real fun was about to begin.

The tanker was across the circle from us at 2,500 feet, having just completed tanking an S-3. Just as we rendezvoused on the A-6, we immediately entered the goo. Gas was down to 2.5. Even though I probably had more practice plugs in the past month than any other pilot in the squadron, trying to tank in turbulent air still proved to be fruitless. We asked the tanker to climb above it, and we reached clear weather at 8,000 feet.

Gas was now at 1.8. We had 0.0 showing on both totalizers since they had been reading 2,000 pounds off the entire flight. The fact that the air was still slightly turbulent and the black juice I was squeezing out of the control stick was beginning to line the inside of the canopy made plugging seem virtually impossible. I've been flying airplanes for over three years now, and I was utterly amazed at how fast gas could burn! All sorts of things were going through my mind. The vision that kept coming back time and time again was the one that had me standing in front of theSkipper trying to explain why I ruined a perfectly good airplane because I couldn't plug. Honestly, that thought scared me much more than barricading or even ejecting!

Gas now down to approximately 1.5–SOP barricade fuel. My RIO had already keyed the radio, ready to say, "We're on our way back for the barricade." At this point the A-6 was dragging us toward the ship and the barricade was about to go up. For some unknown reason the air miraculously smoothed out. I relaxed and then made successful contact with the basket.

Air Ops: "103, are you in?"

103: "Yes, with no flow!"

411: "We don't show you in."

103: "Believe me, we're in!"

411: "We show you in now with good flow. Boss, how much should we give?"

Boss: "How much do you have?"

411: "6.0."

BOSS: "Give him 6.01."

After passing 2.5 on the gas and feeling fat, dumb and happy, the thought of getting aboard seemed almost easy. We left the tanker with 7.0. We proceeded to enter the down-wind, hooked in at four miles and with a few encouraging comments from the LSO, flew an OK 2-wire.

After shutting down and exiting the airplane, I walked down that long passageway to the ready room, thinking that all eyes would be upon me. Walking through the door, the first person I saw was, of course, the Skipper. Half expecting to get chewed out, I wasn't prepared for the Skipper's comments. "Do you know that in your entire naval career, you may never have a more terrifying experience?" he asked. He then told me how proud of me he was for coming through when I had to. What a confidence builder that was!

Lessons Learned:

I learned two major lessons from this experience.

First, don't waste flight time when you could be training. If you've got a few extra minutes off the catapult or before marshal, get practice plugs. It just may save an airplane or even your life.

Second, commanding officers — have faith in your JOs, and give them that boost of confidence whenever you can, especially when they're down. Believe me, it helps.

<u>NOTES:</u>

BUSY TOMCAT CREW
F-14 TOMCAT, UNIT WITHHELD

Name Withheld, January 1988

After completing a night intercept, an F-14 crew suddenly lost their central air data computer (CADC), detail data display panel, tactical information display panel, and had an inertial measurement unit light. The pilot could not reset either the airborne inlet control system or CADC, and noticed he had also lost all trim. The crew decided to return to the carrier.

Since the TACAN was determined to be unreliable, the F-14 requested vectors from the ship. The RIO noticed the wings had swept back to 50 degrees, and the pilot returned them to 20 degrees using emergency wing sweep mode. The pilot also discovered he had no indications of RPM, TIT, fuel flow, AOA or wing sweep. Fuel quantity indications were frozen at 14.7, and to top that off, the F-14 had no exterior lighting.

Ten minutes into the emergency, smoke and fumes entered the cockpit accompanied by the smell of burning rubber. Assuming an environmental control system problem, the pilot selected air source off to secure engine bleed air.

A flash occurred in the rear cockpit, and a fire erupted under the aft panel of the left equipment console. Noting several popped circuit breakers, the RIO secured all electrical equipment. The fire went out within 60 seconds.

The crew declared an emergency and received vectors for the approach, descending to 3,000 feet. They dumped fuel to attain an estimated max trap weight and dirtied up at 25 nm to confirm on speed checks. They found that the speed brakes and slats were out but had no indications of flap position or spoilers being engaged.

The flaps were confirmed down by another F-14 that had joined on the stricken Tomcat to provide a light source for the LSO. The incident pilot had no ACLS needles but flew a Mode III approach to an OK 3-wire arrestment. During the approach, the aircraft was sloppy due to no spoilers or trim, and the pilot had to use full Stick and rudder to make minor corrections on the ball. Post flight inspection revealed standing water under the console had shorted out the left aft cockpit disconnect cannon plug.

It's Okay to Yell "Uncle." We need aggressive aviators in the cockpits, but don't confuse a tiger with a dodo. The young RIO had not been feeling too well due to a bout with flu. The night before, he had cramps and felt queasy. He did not feel much better the following morning, but he ate a light breakfast and lunch. He fooled himself into thinking he felt a little better, though nowhere near 100 percent.

He made his scheduled brief for a two-plane form hop. In the operating area, after some mild manoeuvring, our hero told the pilot he felt sick and Sweaty. He removed his mask and vomited. Though the pilot asked how he was feeling, the RIO allowed the flight to continue until he felt the onset of lightheadedness and disorientation. He locked his harness and replaced his mask, after which he fainted.

The pilot, after failing to get a response from his back-seater, looked in his mirror and saw the RIO immobile, with his head forward. The pilot called his wingman and declared an emergency. The wingman reported the RIO remained motionless.

The F-14 made a straight-in approach and was met by the flight surgeon and ambulance. The RIO remained unconscious even after the canopy was opened. He was placed on a stretcher. He eventually came to, but was confused and was shivering. He had been unconscious for 15 minutes.

Examination at the dispensary revealed the young aviator to be suffering from dehydration and viral illness. He was rehydrated and later released. Locking his harness in flight prevented him from lowering his head, which might have alleviated the lack of blood flow to the brain that brought on his unconsciousness. If he vomited while his mask was on, he might have drowned.

Lessons Learned:

Do not fly when you're sick. Period. End of sentence.

<u>NOTES:</u>

DOWN BUT NOT OUT

TA-4F SKYHAWK, ATTACK SQUADRON FORTY FIVE (VA-45) - BLACKBIRDS

Group Capt. W.R. Donaldson (exchange from RNZAF), March 1988

Squadron Leader Ross Donaldson of the Royal New Zealand Air Force wrote this after an exchange tour with the U.S. Navy. After completing transition to the A-4 Skyhawk, he reported to VA 45. Shortly after joining VA 45, he had this mishap. About a week after the mishap, while recovering in the hospital, he dictated to tape his very interesting story. In edited form it appears below. Group Capt. Donaldson added as a postscript his reflections.

It was my student pilot's first TA-4 low-level cross country, starting at 1,500 feet. If all went well for the first third, we would let down to 500 feet and then 200 feet. The route was from Jacksonville, Florida, up into Georgia, then west, then south to the Florida panhandle, out over the Western Florida coast, then back to Cecil Field. It was a fine day, no low clouds, just scattered cirrus, visibility 16-17 miles in the smog of Jacksonville but increasing as you got away from it.

The flight did not go very well for the student. During the 500-foot portion of the flight, he wandered about 10 miles off track and found only one checkpoint out of five. After some prodding he acknowledged that he was lost, climbed back to 1,500 feet and found out where we were. We were now late, so we increased our speed to 390 knots. We then descended to 200 feet. I was in the back seat with the seat up for visibility, when all of a sudden everything went black, and I sensed I'd been hit very powerfully by something. My head was pushed back against the headrest, and there was a hell of a rushing of air, a lot of noise, and I was blinded. I yelled, "I have control," not knowing what had happened but thinking that either there had been some sort of explosion in the front seat or the canopy had come off and hit me on the head as it went. It was a moment of terror, the only one that I've ever known: doing almost 400 knots at 200 feet, suddenly blind, and with a lot of noise and rushing air. I tried to talk to the student, pulled back on the control column and closed the throttle. I might also have extended the speed brakes; I don't really recall. It all happened pretty fast. I didn't get an answer from the front seat, so I had to assume the worst and that I did indeed have control of the aircraft. In my mind, I had no option but to eject; so I pulled the seat pan handle, and everything worked as advertised. I felt the rocket fire and myself going out of the aircraft. Things felt fine with no great sensations other than the instability of the seat and feeling the rocket stop. Being fairly close to the ground, I had started to operate the harness release and parachute rip cord in case they didn't do so automatically, but then I felt the parachute open cleanly with no shock. There I was, sitting in my parachute harness at an unknown altitude, not knowing really where I was and still completely blind. I removed my oxygen mask but left my helmet on. I heard an accelerating jet engine noise close at hand (more about that later). I was still making a blind parachute descent. I don't think anything else could be more unnerving.

I released the dinghy from its pack; we were near swamp territory here and I didn't want to drown, having just saved my life with the bang seat. I then thought about breaking my ankle on landing as a friend did recently on a sports parachute jump, so I kept my legs and

feet together very tightly and kept saying, "I'm going to hit the ground
. . . now." On about the seventh time, I had just started to say it, when
I fell flat on my backside. My helmet fell over my eyes, and there I
was on my butt, Somewhere in northwest Florida.

I just sat there for a while with my chin in my hands, feeling very
thankful that everything had worked exactly as expected and
thinking about what I would do next. I still couldn't see, which was
very annoying. I took off my torso harness after releasing my parachute, took off my G suit and then sat down again. After a few
minutes or so, I checked out my face. My face was pretty badly
injured and bleeding, so I had to cover it up somehow. The first thing
I thought of was the good old air crew sock. So off with boot and sock,
a good mop around and then both back on as this might be snake
country. At this stage shock must have set in a little, for was shivering.
I gathered my dinghy in (I was still attached to it and my seat pack),
sat in it and pulled the covers over to try to get warm. It was about
1630; sunset would be at about 1720. My right eye started working a
little; when I looked up it was sort of blue, and it was darker when I
looked down. I decided to find my survival radio, so I tied myself to
the dinghy and crawled around looking for the radio. I reasoned that
it must be close. The first thing I found was the empty parachute
pack, so I threw it away and then found it again. This happened
about four times in my circle around the dinghy. I finally found the
survival pack, pulled the dinghy to me and got back in. It then took
me some time to figure out how to undo the pack. I wasn't all that
familiar with it and being blind didn't help. I finally remembered it
had a zipper. I found it, and it all unfolded in front of me. I was
looking for a bandage for my face. It was bleeding quite profusely,
and my flying suit was getting sticky and uncomfortable. Well, I
couldn't find the bandages, for everything was packed in a thick poly-
ethylene bag, rolled over several times and then taped up. I was trying
to tear the plastic and just couldn't do it, so after all that effort to find
the survival pack, I never did get the bandages. I finally undid my
flying suit, taking off my jersey and sort of tying it around my left eye.

I then found the survival radio and managed to get it unwrapped and going. I finally buttoned myself up in the dinghy and just lay there shivering, waiting for something to happen.

While I was waiting heard an aircraft at a distance; however, it did not appear to be looking for me, which was disappointing. I also heard guns, dogs barking and shouting. I yelled at the top of my voice, but nobody appeared to hear me. The most annoying thing was that I didn't know what time it was and couldn't judge the passage of time. I tried counting but soon became bored with that and gave it up. I would also fiddle with the survival pack to try and open it but never did manage that. After what seemed a very long time, a light aircraft came right over me. I heard it coming quite a long way off. It's amazing how keen one's hearing becomes when you're sitting in the middle of the bush, not near anything. I could clearly hear trucks and cars on a highway, which was, in fact, about four miles from where I was. The light aircraft flew past me and then back again, so I presumed it was looking for me because it appeared to be circling around the local area. I tried talking to it on 243 megahertz without success, which wasn't surprising; I found out later it wasn't equipped with UHF. After about four circles it went right overhead at what sounded to be a very low altitude. I waved; the engine note changed, and | then knew that someone had seen me.

The aircraft stayed overhead. I soon heard a truck laboring in a low gear as it approached, and then I heard somebody crashing through undergrowth. I yelled at the top of my voice, "Are you looking for me?" and a voice answered "Where are you?" I said, "Well, I don't really know; I can't see, but I'll keep talking until you find me." Within seconds there was a bloke standing beside me, and the sound of those boots crunching through the undergrowth was very welcome indeed. I said, "Who are you — a farmer or a hunter?" and he said, "I'm neither; I'm a state highway trooper. That's our airplane up there. We found you, and we're going to get you out of here and take you to Tallahassee." "Well, that's jolly good, but where am I?" He replied, "Well, you're sitting in a cornfield." It was a field of maize; the corn had been picked leaving the stalks and leaves. They then brought the truck over to me, and I think the ride out across the cornfield was probably the roughest part of the whole journey from there to the hospital. The paddock had been plowed to put the corn in, and we had to cross the mounds. I bounced all around the cab of the pickup truck until we arrived at a hunting lodge.

The area was all part of a hunting area, and what I had previously heard was a quail hunt in progress. Once at the lodge, I was transferred to a highway patrol car and raced at what seemed a very high speed to the Tallahassee Hospital. When I arrived was given the normal hospital arrival treatment and ended up lying in the casualty department.

At this point my student came into see me, so I think a few lines on his version of the action would now be in order. He had just regained track and was descending down to low-level, when there was a loud bang and a rushing noise from behind his right ear. He felt me pull back on the control column. He said, "You have control," not really knowing what was going on. So he then asked, "What are you doing?" and waited for a reply. By that stage we were in about 30-40 degree climb. The next thing he knew was the canopy blew, and a loud roar and a flash of flame came from the back. He realized that I had ejected but saw no reason to do so himself. In fact, he thought I'd been inadvertently ejected, as a result of the canopy coming off. He recovered from the nose-high, slow-speed attitude, reapplied power (that was the accelerating engine I heard) and turned back to look for me.

In doing that he got into a spiral dive, nearly hit the trees and feeling rather foolish, pulled up and circled once more but didn't see me. We had covered inadvertent ejection in the flight brief, since about 10 days before, the squadron had experienced such an incident when a student had inadvertently jettisoned the canopy. The student did exactly as he had been briefed; he came up on guard, put out a Mayday and turned his IFF to emergency. He had lost all his electrical instruments including his compass and attitude indicator. His standby compass, which was attached to the canopy, had been jettisoned with it. In summary, he was poorly placed to get from point A to B. Tallahassee Center answered his Mayday, and he said it was one of the hardest things of his life trying to explain to the guy what had happened. He said, "Well, my instructor's punched out," and the ATC guy asked, "Are you punching out too?" He replied, "No, no, I'm staying with the airplane." Next was, "Where did your instructor's plane crash?" "Well, he hasn't crashed; it's the same aircraft except he's gone and I'm here." Well, after a couple of minutes of question and answer, the guy on the other end got the picture. They took a fix on the location and guided him to Tallahassee Airport. He landed there with a good crowd of fire tenders and ambulances. He pulled up to the ramp and shut the engine down, which stopped very quickly. The engine was very badly FODed with bird because that's what we'd had, a very solid bird strike. He got out of the aircraft, was escorted across to the control tower and was told that a state highway patrol plane was standing by and would he please get in and point out where his instructor had ejected. Fortunately, he had the presence of mind to ring the squadron first. They were pretty inured to this sort of thing because unfortunately, mishaps were not an uncommon feature of squadron life. He then got into the little airplane and toddled off. It was now nearly dusk when they picked up the parachute and dinghy lying in the cornfield and directed the highway patrolmen on the ground to where I was. The rest you know from my side of the story.

From then on I was in the hands of the medics. They did as much as they possibly could and patched me up to the best of their considerable ability.

The mishap investigation determined that we had been hit by a mallard drake - a male duck. It struck the aircraft just on the line where the canopy joins the metal on the right hand side about abeam of the front pilot's shoulder. It then made its way up the canopy slightly and broke through. At that stage presumably most of its lateral velocity became longitudinal, and the thing moved and hit me on the left side of my face. Another duck went down the engine. As far as any of the U.S. aviation agencies are aware, it was the first occasion when a bird had entered a jet aircraft's canopy from the side. The duck must have been moving at a fair rate of speed to actually get right through the canopy at that particular point. Looking back on it, if I was faced with the same problem again, of being blinded and not able to talk to anyone or not knowing if there was anyone alive in the front seat, I would do exactly what I did on that occasion. I believe the only thing I omitted to do was to turn on my strobe light - that may have helped the search team if it had been later in the evening. And, come to think of it, I would get to know my survival gear a bit more intimately, especially how to open the container!

15 Years On - Reflections on an Incident In One's Life

There was a preface to the story that you just read, and it contains a lesson for all of us.

It was squadron (and Navy attack community) policy that all low-levels be "chased" with the student and the instructor in separate aircraft. It was believed that this increased student confidence and allowed him to get on with the navigation, freed from the presence and distraction of another crew member.

On that Tuesday, my student and were detailed for a 0700 brief and a 0800 launch in two A-4Cs. One aircraft did not come up on time, so the launch was postponed until 1000 hours. Preflight, start and taxi were normal until we got to the "final checker," the last quality assurance inspection, which was conducted outside the flight line area. A severe hydraulic leak on my aircraft was detected, so we both returned to the ramp and shut down. Maintenance and Ops consulted, and I was assigned a TA4F as chase replacement, but it wouldn't be available until midday.

At about 1230 we mounted up again, and this time the student's aircraft was unserviceable on startup — I can't recall the reason, but the Charlie was a recalcitrant aircraft at times. The diagnosis for a replacement was poor, and as the mission Instructor Pilot, I was given the option of flying the low-level dual in a T-bird or cancelling out. My hunger for hours prevailed, and that's how we and a couple of ducks were predestined to meet a few hours later.

Lessons Learned:

On reflection, I suppose someone was trying to tell me that it wasn't a good idea to fly that day, but I wasn't listening to the "whispers." I was determined to fly.

Perhaps there are times when you're pressing on, eager to get the job done, when you don't hear the "whispers" loudly enough to make you pause and reconsider what you're doing. Listen for the "whispers" — it could be your professional conscience calling — or it might be someone else.

NOTES:

HARD TO STOP

A-4C SKYHAWK, UNIT WITHHELD

Name Withheld, Date Unknown

After an early breakfast of one glass of juice, an A-4C pilot briefed for a two-plane cross-country flight. The flight was to be filed IFR, and he was to fly wing.

About 25 minutes after takeoff, the flight was clear of clouds and level at FL 290 when the pilot experienced a loud, high-frequency tone in his earphones. He turned down the radar altimeter and radar obstruction warning volumes, but the tone persisted. He turned down the UHF volume, and the tone ceased.

The AJB-3 and RMI were noted to be inoperative. He communicated his difficulties to the flight leader using a HEFOE signal. The flight leader elected to return to Homebase and descended to FL 220 where the wingman deployed his emergency generator. The UHF volume was then successfully turned up without the high frequency tone, enabling the wingman to communicate by radio with the flight leader. The AJB-3 and RMI were still inoperative.

During descent to Homebase, the flight entered an overcast layer at 9,000 feet but was VFR between layers at 7,000. After reentering clouds, while continuing descent, the wingman experienced vertigo.

The flight was in and out of the clouds at 1500 feet prior to glide slope interception. Airspeed on GCA final was 140 knots with speed brakes in. The leader called the runway in sight at 5 miles and was cleared to land on Runway 1 R (12,000 feet long). He passed the lead to the wingman and went around.

Just before the wingman touched down, he observed a very low ball and added power, but overcorrected. He landed fast 700-800 feet past the mirror (located 750 feet from the end of the runway). He commenced aerodynamic braking then lowered the nose with 6,500 feet remaining.

At 6,000 feet, the flaps were raised and braking was commenced (AFC 272 not incorporated). He applied light braking until airspeed was below 100 knots, then moderate braking. With 4,000 feet remaining at 95 knots, the pilot still thought he had control and would be able to stop on the runway.

Approaching the abort gear (1,500 feet from the end of the runway), the pilot noted less than 80 knots and still thought he could stop the aircraft. Braking was discontinued as the aircraft crossed the abort gear, then reapplied. The pilot then suddenly realized he wouldn't be able to stop on the runway. He shut down the engine and stood on the brakes, but to no avail. The aircraft continued off the end of the runway, past the overrun, and stopped 1385 feet off the runway's end. There was no aircraft damage but investigations revealed the starboard interior console lighting rheostat and wiring had burned out causing the AJB-3 and RMI to fail.

Lessons Learned:

The CO, in his endorsement, stated:

"After this incident, functional checks of the aircraft involved did not reveal any brake system malfunction. The aircraft was test flown and landed without difficulty. It can only be concluded that the pilot did not use correct landing and stopping techniques.

It is likely that anxiety, complacency, and a lack of knowledge all played a part in this incident during which the A-4 rolled approximately 11,800 feet before stopping. That such an event could occur, even though the squadron held a 2-day comprehensive safety stand-down only 2 months earlier, is notable. Also, frequent NATOPS lectures and safety examinations have been conducted; and all pilots have been closely observed during familiarization flights.

It has been emphasized many times that all pilots should set up their approaches to land on speed, on the end of the runway. This was not accomplished in this case. No wave-off was attempted, even though there was adequate fuel available for a go-around; and the field was VFR. Aerodynamic braking is not mentioned in NATOPS for any condition, and neither is raising the flaps unless there is a strong crosswind. At the time of landing, there was a 20-degree crosswind at 8 knots.

The pilot did not allow the nose-wheel to fall through normally and consequently did not hold full forward stick after landing. He failed to correctly correlate aircraft speed and runway distance remaining and did not use available runway abort gear. That the pilot did not eat a proper breakfast before the flight is a possible contributing factor in the form of hypoglycaemia.

This incident was discussed a short time after it happened at an All Pilots Meeting. NATOPS procedures for all types of landings and proper braking techniques were extensively reviewed.

Constant vigilance regarding creeping complacency and the adequacy of a squadron's training program is necessary. A part of the program must be devoted to keeping pilots aware of the inherent dangers involving a lack of knowledge of normal and emergency NATOPS procedures, as well as the dangers of non adherence to these procedures."

NOTES:

I CAN HACK IT

F-14 TOMCAT, STRIKE FIGHTER SQUADRON ONE NINE FIVE (VFA-195) - DAMBUSTERS

Lt. James R. Knapp, May 1988

Once again it is time to renew my night qual. No problem - a Case III launch and recovery with a few night intercepts thrown in for good measure. One trap tonight and another tomorrow night and "presto!" – I'm a qual.

In preparation for the at-sea period, I had flown six bounce periods (right about average for us forward-deployed kind of guys). True, I hadn't flown the first six days out for a lot of reasons, but I had two day traps and one touch-and-go in the last couple of days. I felt ready to go. Besides, because of some great CONUS TAD, my last night trap was only 5% months ago.

"Whattya mean, "No gas for the CAP'" Don't they know we're 'real world' here?" I ask the duty officer just before I walk to my jet.

"Hey, back off! I'm just the talking dog here. Air Ops is the villain," the SDO replies in an injured tone.

Well, that's just great. I guess the gas would have been gravy anyway. I can make it without tanking. Let's see, one little gripe about fuel venting while transferring the drops if the internal bag is full. No sweat! I'll just hold the transfer until I'm down to 7K internal. Other than that, the trusty Hornet is 4.0.

Jeez, do I have my day visor down, or is it really this dark? Good preflight, start is normal, all checks – great, ready to go. Taxi up to cat 2. Roger the weight board . . . oops, dropped my flashlight. Luckily, it's an idiot flashlight, tied to my torso with about 9 feet of nylon line. Keep taxiing, turn left, reel in the flashlight and hope it doesn't get caught in the ejection handle; double check takeoff checks. Tension! Everything looks good. Lights on. Rats! Forgot to turn on the HUD. Ooof! Airborne. Airspeed looks good. Instruments working OK. Wonder how my attitude's doing?

God or the Air Boss thinks I should "Keep it climbing!"

I take the suggestion to heart and pull it out of afterburner and raise the gear as I'm passing 2,500 feet.

My pulse starts to return to normal as I reach my assigned CAP station. I'll just let George fly her for a while. Dang, climbing and still IMC at 22K. Level off and still IMC at 28K. I'll climb up to look for VMC a little later when I'm lighter. This could be a long night. Those strobe lights are really annoying in the goo; I'll just turn them off for a while.

"Bingo! Bingo!" Why'd they pick a computer voice that sounds like a female Wehrmacht commando? Oh, well, at least she's right. Seven thousand internal – time to transfer the drops. Both drops transferring, something's going right tonight.

Guess I'll try the strobes again. Great, not as bad as before. Looks like "vapes" coming off the vertical stabs; that's Strange. Damn! That's fuel! Transfer off. Too late, the damage is done – 800 pounds above my fuel ladder to 1,200 pounds below in a heartbeat.

Dandy, just dandy. At least I'm light enough to climb out of this soup. Still IMC at 35K. Where's the icing level anyway? Wish I'd listened more closely to the weather brief. Oh, well, I can hack it up here. I just hope this vertigo goes away soon.

When I check into marshal with my fuel state, their response is an incredulous, "Say again fuel state!" I repeat my state, and the signal is "Tank." I could probably hack it, but why turn down gas? Maybe because I've got a solid case of vertigo and I haven't night tanked since my last night trap. I'm probably going to remember this hop.

Departure vectors me to my tanker just as he calls "We're at 5K climbing to 7K for weather." I arrive at 7K and see that, yep, he did it; he found the weather. At a quarter mile, the tanker disappears as we go IMC yet again. Breaking out, I join just before we enter the clouds again. We're in and out of the stuff as the basket moves randomly in the cross currents, maddeningly close to, but never on, my probe. Twelve rounds of Sparring follow, and the basket is way ahead on all fight cards. A timely head fake surprises the basket, and I get my allotted gas, not to mention a raging case of vertigo.

Having hacked the tanking, I check back into marshal and decel smartly through 160 knots as I copy my instructions. Damn! Where's my scan?

Twenty-five miles and three minutes to push – no hill for a stepper. An idle 5g turn miraculously puts me at 248 knots pushing "on time." The problem, I fully realize, is that I left what little scan I had back on the tanker. I've had no time to mentally prepare myself for this last crucial phase of the flight.

Somehow, I successfully chase the ILS needles to a decent start. I go a little low on the ball call and squeak on some power to correct. Meatball, lineup, AOA. Meatball, needles – needles show me high. Oops! Lined up left now. Squeak off some power for the high, make the lineup correction, anticipate the burble . . .

"Power back on," a calm, confident LSO voice crackles over the UHF.

Get outta here! I can spot the deck with the best of them. I'm still high!

"Power . . . WAVE OFF!" a new LSO voice, and this one's scared. Me too!

The ball's red and falling. Full power from the Hornet's two F-404 engines saves me, but the l-wire cuts my wave off embarrassingly short. My feet beat a Staccato rhythm on the rudder pedals as my knees shake uncontrollably during the taxi up the deck.

Lessons Learned:

Later in the reflective calm of the ready room, I review the mistakes that led to my most unforgettable night pass.

Given the known fuel-system discrepancy, I should have monitored my fuel more closely and caught it long before 2,000 pounds had been irretrievably lost.

I didn't listen to the weather brief close enough to determine what altitudes would be best to work during the course of the hop.

During the final portion of the hop, my "I can hack it" attitude set me up for a bad pass. I first accepted a bad tanking altitude knowing full well that there was clear weather just above us.

Secondly, I accepted an unreasonable approach time because I didn't want to hold up the recovery. The end result was a poor approach that the LSO had to dig me out of. Fortunately, the only damage was a lowered landing grade average and a slightly more colorful call sign – all-in-all, a fairly cheap lesson.

As pilots-in-command, it's our responsibility to control as many factors as possible to assure the safe completion of our assigned mission. A two or three-minute delay was probably all I would have needed to straighten out my head and make a safe, normal approach. Remember, everyone out there is trying to kill you – they don't need your help.

<u>NOTES:</u>

ARE YOU READY TO BE ON-SCENE COMMANDER?

A-4E SKYHAWK FLOWN BY CDR. WELLER, COMPOSITE SQUADRON FIVE (VC-5) - KC-130 (NAMES & UNIT WITHHELD)

LCdr. Scott A. Beaton, May 1988

A KC-130 was on station at FL210 for an afternoon tanker mission 50 nm east of Butterworth Air Base in Malaysia. The crew of the KC-130, whose call sign was Plaid 21, topped off Checker 01, an A-4E. The refuelling had gone smoothly in a small clear area surrounded by thunderstorms, which are standard during the monsoon season in the afternoon. Two minutes after the A-4 departed, Plaid 21 received a call from Cdr. Gary Weller, the Skyhawk pilot.

"I've got a 20 percent low oil light and would like you to follow me to Butterworth to divert."

The A-4 then quickly descended beneath the thunderstorms that were in all quadrants. Four minutes later, Checker 01 called,

"I've got smoke and fumes in the cockpit and a chugging engine. It looks like I'm going to have to jump out."

Due to the clouds, altitude separation and distance between the two aircraft, Plaid 21 had lost sight of the A-4. Maj. Paul Chase, the pilot in command of the tanker, called Cdr. Weller for a TACAN posit.

Since the KC-130 crew could not see the ejection and would have to descend IFR, they stayed at FL210 for several minutes to ensure they would not inadvertently fly into Cdr. Weller's chute or his Skyhawk. After descending through the clouds, Maj. Chase found a clear area in a valley but had to remain less than 1,000 feet AGL to stay clear of the clouds and avoid the surrounding mountains. The KC-130 had to make extremely tight turns at low altitude to stay in the valley and clear of clouds because the weather was rapidly deteriorating.

Seventeen minutes after Cdr. Weller's ejection, the tanker made radio contact with him. Cdr. Weller had passed out upon ejection and sustained major injuries when he landed. To keep the commander alert and coherent, Maj. Chase recounted what had happened and asked about his injuries. Cdr. Weller replied, "I can't move anything except my left arm."

Cdr. Weller's skyward view was obstructed because his chute was suspended in small saplings 8 to 10 feet above him.

Major Chase asked for a long count for a UHF/DF cut, then started to make passes in that portion of the valley. After a few passes, Cdr. Waller called, "Mark on top" based on the sound of the tanker's engines. During the ensuing hard turn, the crew sighted the downed pilot's chute.

Forty minutes into the SAR effort, the first Royal Malaysian Air Force helicopter (Chopper 01) checked in, five minutes out. Unfortunately, the helo ran into a wall of thunderstorms and had to run 60 miles south before they could find a hole to cut through and transit back up the valley. Twenty minutes later, there was still no sign of any helos. Cdr. Weller was now fading in and out of consciousness. Also, as the Sun began to set and the weather continued to deteriorate. (The storm system was classified as a weather warning less than 30 minutes after Cdr. Weller was finally rescued.)

Finally, another helo, Chopper 55D, reported on scene from the north. The pilot was reluctant to land, however, after hearing about Cdr. Weller's injuries, because he had no medical personnel aboard. Concerned for the commander's safety and the deteriorating weather, MSgt. John Merchant, the navigator, strongly encouraged, then convinced–as perhaps only a Marine Corps master sergeant can– Chopper 55D to land and assist Cor. Weller.

Within 10 minutes, Chopper 01 reported inbound. MSgt. Merchant vectored Chopper 01 in and coordinated the positioning of both helicopters. Five minutes later, Chopper 01's SAR/medical team was on the ground with the injured A-4 pilot.

Because of Cdr. Weller's condition, the SAR team decided to hoist him aboard with a locally manufactured, hoist capable metal stretcher instead of his D-Ring. This procedure worked perfectly and prevented further injuries. Chopper 01 then took Cor. Weller to Butterworth.

Meanwhile, Maj. Chase coordinated with Chopper 55D to secure the crash site, and mark the location of the wreckage and the rescue scene for the mishap inspection team and salvage efforts. As darkness fell, the crew of Plaid 21 turned east, negotiated another wall of thunderstorms and returned to base.

During the ejection sequence, Cdr. Weller suffered a separated shoulder, a fractured collarbone and shoulder blade, five fractured ribs, a partially collapsed lung, and was in severe shock.

His right arm was also temporarily paralyzed due to major nerve damage in the arm and shoulder.

Lessons Learned:

Without Major Chase and the crew of Plaid 21, the weather alone would have prevented a successful rescue until the following day.

The superior airmanship, cool headwork, determination and superb crew coordination displayed by Plaid 21 were the key to rescuing Cdr. Weller.

LCdr. Beaton
A TAR (Training and Administration of Reserves), assigned to CVWR-30 (Carrier Air Wing Reserve Thirty). He was the VC-885 Program Manager on detachment in Malaysia at the time of this incident. VC-885 is the Reserve Augmentation Unit of VC-5.

NOTES:

A-4 WITH AFTERBURNER

A-4 SKYHAWK, VC13 FLEET COMPOSITE SQUADRON THIRTEEN (VC-13) - SAINTS

LCol Craig A. Grover, June 1988

Occasionally, while getting drilled by some Tomcat driver on a DACT (Dissimilar Air Combat Training) mission, I've recalled my old Crusader days when a slight outboard movement of the throttle provided an extra 6,000 pounds of thrust. Give me an afterburner in the Skyhawk and I'd really show them some thrust to weight. Well, one day, my dream came true – only it turned out to be a nightmare.

My copilot and I were flying as a bogey wingman on a multi-plane DACT event on the Yuma Tactical Aircrew Combat Training System (TACTS) range. While orbiting at 10,000 feet after our first engagement, the copilot heard an odd engine noise, scanned the instruments and noted the oil pressure at zero. He told me and recommended an immediate turn toward MCAS Yuma. Looking at my own gauge and confirming the problem, I complied quickly.

During the turn toward Yuma, we divided responsibilities. The copilot handled communications, coordination with a chase aircraft, and reviewed the pocket checklist (PCL). I set the power at 88 percent per NATOPS, changed he squawk to emergency, and pointed the aircraft toward the approach end of the duty parallel runways, 03 Left and Right. My copilot switched to approach, declared an emergency, and read off – over the ICS – the procedures for oil pressure failure and precautionary approach.

During our long trip to Yuma (10 minutes), our oil pressure remained at zero; the oil quantity remained normal. As you might expect, the engine began making angry complaints including a grinding noise and moderate to severe vibrations. It took no time to figure out we were in deep trouble. With a successful landing on the duty runway in serious doubt, we decided to risk a tail wind landing — winds 350 at 10 – and proceeded to the closest set of suitable runways, 21 Left and Right.

Fifteen miles east of Yuma, we encountered slight rpm fluctuations and severe vibrating, grinding, moaning, groaning, shuddering and a few other things. I'm not denying that some of the shaking may have originated from inside the cockpit. We discussed the possibility of ejection, switched to Tower and continued on our way.

About 10-12 miles from the runway, the engine rpm started slowly rolling back. The chase aircraft reported sparks coming from the tailpipe. What a sickening feeling – like the world was about to fall out from under us. However, the engine reluctantly continued to provide thrust, so we pressed on. We modified the normal precautionary approach glide slope (1.5 miles per 1,000 feet of altitude) in favor of a steeper, faster approach. We were coming in offset about 60 degrees from the runway heading, so when we got to the airfield, we would still have a 60 degree turn to make. There was a shorter 6,000-foot runway straight ahead that we had not considered, but fate would later eliminate that option. We were planning to land on the longest runway, but keeping our options open, we requested both 21 Left and Right.

As we started down, we were definitely high – about a 1,000-foot-per-mile glide slope. Since I did not want to give up any airspeed before its time, I dropped the gear at 250 knots (25 knots above NATOPS gear speed). Normally I would feel guilty about such an act, but at the time, I did not want to risk any additional load on the bearings that the speed brakes or a pull-up manoeuvre might cause. Initially, I used three-quarter flaps to control glide slope. However, I raised them back up as engine rpm decreased through 80 percent. Our airspeed stabilized at about 210 knots.

There comes a time when an engine decides enough is enough. As rpm decreased through 70 percent, the fuel control couldn't decide whether to provide fuel flow for the 80 percent throttle setting or the 70 percent engine speed; so, it did both. Large fuel flow fluctuations and engine surges resulted. The copilot, not missing a thing, called for manual fuel. I was out of ideas, so I complied. When switching to manual, I did not match throttle position with rpm as NATOPS requires because of another NATOPS consideration: leaving the throttle set following oil-pressure failure. Is this one of those gray areas?

Well, at last my dream came true—an A-4 with an afterburner. Manual fuel gave us stabilized engine performance for a few precious seconds, at the expense of an extremely over-temped engine. Ground observers stated there was an orange glow coming from our tailpipe, like an afterburner. But stabilized engine performance and slightly increased thrust gave us enough energy to make the airfield. After a few seconds, the engine rpm started rolling back again, but at a reduced rate and without surges.

Although we were coming down over farmland as we approached the field, we noted air station buildings ahead and to the left, and civilian air terminal buildings ahead and to the right. We were in a box. Ejecting now meant endangering people on the ground. What happened to the ejection option that the precautionary approach is supposed to preserve? We still had airspeed to make the left runway and maybe the right. However, the engine was still rolling back and, if rpm dropped below 20 percent, we would lose hydraulics. And if we lost hydraulics, we would lose flight controls. And if we lost flight controls, we would have no control over where the aircraft landed, or crashed. So, we discussed disconnecting the hydraulics – which meant flying with cables only.

Then came the airliner. Out of nowhere, a civilian jet rolled onto the concrete directly in front of us. The airliner had just landed on the 6,000 foot cross runway that I mentioned earlier. Now ejection really looked bad. With flying speed still at 210 knots, we decided to press on a little further, if not to land, then at least to turn and avoid the airliner. Suddenly, no generator! As advertised, the generator dropped off the line at 45 percent engine rpm. The copilot deployed the RAT, and electrical power was restored. The engine was decelerating more rapidly now. As rpm decayed to 30 percent, I pulled the hydraulic flight control disconnect handle. The disconnect was normal and provided stiff, but usable controls. With adrenaline levels high, I had no trouble moving the stick.

The engine continued its rollback, and the right runway no longer looked attainable at our steep descent angle. The left runway still looked good, so we decided to try for it. With 10 percent rpm and flames out of the tailpipe as reported by the chase plane (we saw no fire warning light), we began a 45 degree angle of bank turn for 21 Left. I had both hands on the stick for control, and the copilot – God bless him — had both hands on the lower handle just in case I couldn't maintain control.

Unfortunately, here at the most critical part of our approach, we could not use the ICS without freeing up a much needed hand. Had I been smart, I would have selected "hot-mike" early in the approach.

As we came around for the final turn, I felt a wing drop, and I temporarily took out some of the angle of bank, which produced a sizeable overshoot. Having had enough flying for the day, and not wishing to negotiate another airborne turn with a seized engine and manual flight controls, I set the aircraft down at 200 knots on the asphalt just off the right side of 21 Left. We rolled on the runway at 190 knots and 5 percent rpm, with 5,000 feet of runway remaining. I got on the brakes, shut off the throttle and started fumbling with the manual fuel shutoff lever. Seeing the longfield gear signs, the copilot called for, and lowered, the hook. Then, to our dismay, we looked forward and saw the longfield arresting gear derigged. Time for more brakes.

Then, out of nowhere, up popped a carrier-type barricade at the end of the runway. The barricade had been installed one week ago for the F-21s used by VMFT-401, but I had not known about it. At first, it gave me a warm feeling to know we were being looked after. Then, I decided we'd really have a warm feeling if we couldn't get the canopy up or off while on fire in the barricade. It was then I found out how strong my feet really were.

We blew both tires 80 feet from the end of the runway and stopped three feet from the barricade. My attempt at manually pumping up the canopy was too slow for the back-seater who was sitting much closer to the smoking engine; he blew the canopy. I knew they put that jettison handle there for a reason. It sure works quicker than a hand pump.

After the copilot reminded me to safe the ejection seat with the head knocker, we quickly egressed. The copilot beat me out by several seconds. For a few minutes we watched the Yuma crash crew do an outstanding job of putting out brake and engine fires. Then we were carted off to the dispensary to donate blood (seven tubes) and suffer the various indignities of a complete physical.

Post-mishap inspection revealed heat damage to the tail section, including the LOX compartment and rudder cables. The engine turbine section had been cut through by a turbine wheel and was being held together by exterior lines. The tailpipe had collapsed and was burned through in several places. Obviously, the aircraft had been close to exploding. Fortunately, the heat shield had done its job and contained the spread of fire in flight.

The cause? One loose, un-safety-wired bolt in the engine accessory case had worked its way past a screen, had been Sucked into the scavenge side of the main oil pump, had jammed an impeller, and had sheered the pump Spline, causing instantaneous loss of oil pressure.

Would I make the same choices in a future situation? Will I eject when the engine gives its first signs of imminent failure? I hope I never find out. What would you do? I've heard it said, "Know when to go, then go." But the ejection decision may not be that clear-cut. There may be people on the ground to consider. You may be feet dry over hostile territory. Or maybe, as in our case, the engine holds together just long enough to sucker you into attempting a landing. Know your options. But, most importantly, don't let our success lure you into a box from which you can't escape. Remember, ejections are more than 90 percent successful. Can you say the same for attempts at landing without an engine?

Lessons Learned:

- Landing with a seized engine is no fun.
- NATOPS does not cover every contingency. Some compound emergencies may have conflicting guidance.
- An A-4 can still fly with a seized engine, but not far.
- A-4 disconnected flight controls work, but are uncomfortable in a steep turn (such as the abeam precautionary approach profile). Following engine seizure, manual controls could be used to reach a clear area or to effect a pull-up prior to ejection.
- A-4 manual fuel works fine, but matching throttle with rpm prior to switching to manual is important. If that cannot be done, expect heat damage.
- I've heard jet engines can run 30 minutes without oil. Maybe so, but don't count on it.
- Know your NATOPS procedures. Know your options.
- If you are not certain which runway you will land on during an emergency, ask Tower to clear all the runways.
- Use "hot-mike" when things get hot.

- Two crew members are better than one for handling compound emergencies as long as they work together. Define your roles.
- A-4s don't need afterburners, except in our case.

Finally, I want to thank my copilot, LCdr. Scott Beaton, for staying with me.

Few can dispute the outstanding airmanship shown by LCdrs. Grover and Beaton in this extremely close call. Inevitably, though, this incident will bring up age old questions:

Should the crew have stayed with the aircraft or should they have ejected? Did they violate NATOPS by failing to eject?

Navy policy concerning flameout approaches and aircraft on fire is straightforward:

Flameout approaches will not be flown unless it is impossible, or impractical to eject.

And if there is a verified fire in an aircraft, eject.

This mishap fell into a gray area that wasn't covered by either of those policies. The engine lost power, but did not flameout.

Sparks came out of the engine, but there was no indication of a sustained fire until prior to touch down.

In situations which are not covered by NATOPS, we have to rely on the pilot to exercise their best judgement based on their experience and unique perspective. The pilot must make an instantaneous decision, and it's not fair to second-guess him based on extensive retrospective analysis in the calm of the ready room or safety desk.

This in no way contradicts or changes official Navy policy. If the engine has failed and can't be restarted, eject. If your aircraft has a verified fire, eject. If you have a situation in between these extremes, use your best judgment. That's what separates naval aviators from robots.

NOTES:

TRUST ME, I KNOW WHAT I'M DOING

F-14 TOMCAT, FIGHTER SQUADRON ONE ONE FOUR (VF-114) - AARDVARKS

Lt. Mike Dunn, June 1988

"God, how I love gunning the new guy's brains out," our second-tour pilot screams over the Tomcat's ICS.

"Let's set up one more engagement before heading to marshal."

His RIO, also a new guy, keys the mike,

"Yo, Mr. experienced pilot, I show us on our fuel ladder right now. Maybe we oughta just check out with strike and save a little gas."

"That's a big negative, you. This guy's a grape, and besides, one more minute of burner won't take much gas anyhow, Besides it's gonna be a pinky trap. Trust me, I know what I'm doing."

"Hey, that was a pretty decent first move by the new guy — let's light 'em up and go for the moon."

Three minutes and 3,500 pounds of fuel later, two F-14s are driving toward the stack.

"Go ahead and check us in first, we're just a little skosh on JP-5. We'll be back in the ready room before the roll 'em." "99 Barbwire, Marshal, your signal is max conserve, the launch has been delayed."

"Terrific," barks our experienced hero.

"This is all we need. At least we're at the bottom of the stack, and we'll be aboard first. Hope they wait on us before firing up the popcorn machine."

"What do you think about asking for a little opportunity fuel?" his rookie RIO asks.

"Naw, we'll probably push any minute now." Two more Delta 5s and our hero dumps the fighter's nose. Next stop, USS Boat. At four miles, his RIO is up hot mike.

"I got us a hundred feet low."

"No problem, pal. This scud layer at 1,200 feet is the reason why. I'm trying to get a peek at home plate. Don't want to blow this first one. It's getting dark."

"Still showing us low at 2¾ miles," the RIO comments.

"I've got good bullseye. . .this one's suitcased. I don't need a self-contained tonight."

At three-quarters of a mile, our hero is on and on.

"Roger ball, Tomcat, wave this one off. Fouled deck."

"Fouled deck! You gotta be kidding me," he says while adding military power to his jet and climbing back to 1,200 feet.

"We were in there. What's going on down there?" His RIO makes the abeam call. Their state is tank plus one, but our hero convinces the rookie to inflate the gas total by a grand or so.

"Trust me, I know what I'm doing. I don't feel like tanking tonight."

CATCC finds a hole in the marshal stack and turns the fighter in at six miles.

"1 11, Tomcat ball, 3.9."

"Crap," our experienced pilot thinks out loud. "Now they know our real fuel state. Hope the skipper isn't watching the plat. No biggee. We're almost aboard."

"Hook skip! No way." The Tomcat climbs away from the carrier deck, turning crosswind on his second trip to the penalty box.

"111, Approach, your signal is tank. Hook up, gear up. Join 413 overhead at angels 12. You are authorized 2.5."

The cockpit is silent, except for the buzz of the environmental control system.

"Two-point five. What's the point? We'll burn more than that getting to the tanker," our hero complains. His RIO is Silent, searching his scope for 413.

"Got him, 30 right at four miles. Closure is 150 knots."

"Not a problem," our veteran coolly replies.

It wasn't the most beautiful tanker rendezvous he'd flown. They joined on the A-7. The tanker was having some trouble with his buddy store. Finally, they were plugged and receiving. At 4.0, the F-14's fuel totalizer stopped moving.

"How about a few more gallons," our second-tour aviator begged.

"Let me recycle," came the Corsair's response. "I think I may be sour."

"Oh, God. This can't be happening to me. A fouled deck wave-off, a bolter and no gas."

Two more stabs at the basket. No gas. Our hero subconsciously rolled the temperature control rheostat down a couple of notches. It had somehow become very warm in the Tomcat.

Random vectors and a quick descent took our hero and his RIO to a three-mile final.

"Yeah, yeah. . . checklist complete." The experienced pilot searched his VDI for the ILS bullseye that would guide him to a good start. The fuel gauge showed plus or minus 100 pounds of 2.6 just before the ball call.

Our hero's left hand clicked the throttles to the military stop as the huge fighter touched down on the tiny deck.

"Bolter, Bolter," the LSO said. Again, it was silent in the airplane. "111, Paddles, check your hook down."

The second-tour pilot felt his heart in his throat as his eyes fell upon the hook handle. It was up. He hadn't noticed the flashing indexers on that last approach. He'd forgotten to lower the hook after tanking. The experienced fighter pilot and the new RIO completed the landing checklist just as the right fuel low light flashed, and 1.9 showed on the fuel totalizer.

The Tomcat slammed onto the flight deck 30 feet aft of the one wire, despite two power calls from Paddles. Both low-fuel lights glowed brightly as the jet was tugged to a standstill. They were aboard.

The Tomcat was parked and chained before our hero noticed his legs. They stopped shaking about half way to the ready room. His new RIO didn't say much until the two aviators entered the maintenance control spaces. The skipper was already there. The junior RIO looked up at the second tour pilot.

"I'll let you explain it to the CO," he said.

"I trust you. You know what you're doing."

Lessons Learned:

Don't be cocky. The new guy might just have picked up something you missed!

NOTES:

ANOTHER NIGHT ADVENTURE
F-14 TOMCAT, FIGHTER SQUADRON TWO ONE
(VF-21) - FREELANCERS

LCdr. Rick Berg, March 1991

How could a routine, night FCLP (Field Carrier Landing Practice) hop at our home field turn into one of those nights in a barrel? Quite easily. It was time for that check in the block before getting underway in WESTPAC. The plan called for a hot switch, hot pump, launch into the GCA (ground-controlled approach) box for a quick instrument refresher. Then we would slide over into the old FCLP pattern to satisfy the bounce requirement for a refresher CQ the following week.

We had briefed and slid with the flight schedule into the late evening as seasonal fog hung off the coastline just a few miles to the west. After the hot switch, we couldn't refuel since the pits were closed because of new, shorter hours to reduce station operating costs. No problem, 6.8 on the fuel was enough for a few laps around the pattern to make the LSOs happy.

I held short, waiting for the tower's evaluation of the new weather which had gone down below the field's VFR minimums. Our minds drifted away, organizing the week-before-cruise-get-everything-done game plan. Twenty minutes slipped by when the tower announced, "Weather now 1,000 scattered, variable, broken. Visibility three miles. Tomcats holding short, want to try it?" Sure, why not! I thought. It still looks clear to the west and it would really help ops if we got this flight out. Besides, if it's not workable, we can just full-stop and try again tomorrow night.

After takeoff and a turn downwind, the aircraft attitude display (VDI) went blank and retired for the evening. Well, that's what standby gyros are for.

At 600 feet AGL, abeam, paddles lost sight of us while our "ground gauges" vanished. Great, I thought, they always preach an instrument turn off the abeam but I'm used to cheating a little, especially without the VDI. The hairs on the back of my neck went up at the 135 as I levelled my wings and climbed out of the scud layer to take it around.

"Tower, 206 requests a full stop on the next pass. The bounce is not workable."

"Roger, 206, you're cleared number one on the right."

OK, next pass, we'll just stay below this stuff and keep a tally on the field. We enjoyed a good case of vertigo off the abeam, trying to remain VMC, scanning the instruments and the faint stream of cars going down the expressway right below us. Then, we went IMC at the 90.

That water-tower-at-the-90 gouge that always saved our pattern was now our adversary. The weather back doored us from the east (which never happens at this field), clobbering the approach end. Maybe we launched into a sucker hole. After levelling the wings and climbing out of the scud again, we asked for vectors to a GCA full stop.

A couple of laps in the "delta" went by as we calculated our time remaining before we had to divert. I wished we had started with a normal bounce load.

"206, looks like it will be a while," said the tower.

"Approach is saturated."

"Tower, we've got 15 minutes before we have to divert Over the hill."

We wondered how approach could be saturated when our GCA box was empty. It turned out that the controllers had scaled down to a skeleton crew in the late evening — again, reducing operating costs.

We didn't know that the horde of bingo diverts inbound off the CV and commercial airline traffic were getting higher priority. OK, decision time.

"Tower, if we can't get vectors for a GCA now, we request a divert."

"206, roger. Approach still can't take you now. Stand by for your divert routing."

Ever get that helpless, boxed-in feeling as your options slip away? We did more laps in the delta and still no clearance. Are those guys home? The inevitable bingo fuel (padded a bit) arrived. Frustrated, we left NAS Homefield on a bingo profile east to the desert and earned a night in the Splinterville BOQ (Bachelor Officer Quarters).

I wished the VDI would reset and I wondered why operating on the beach had to be that hard. I realized that I had not adjusted from the CV operating environment, which had become so routine during the previous six months during workups. At sea, your rep in air ops faithfully lobbies for your spot in the CCA pattern or buys you a little more flying time with a tanker. After getting aboard in poor weather, at night, with a pitching deck, it's easy to play down the hazards of shore operations.

We called approach on our climb and were greeted unexpectedly with, "206, turn right, heading 150 degrees, and descend to 3,000 for a hook to final." One more hard look at our fuel determined that we had just enough for one approach. I was uneasy about not keeping a little in the hip pocket and possibly letting our desire to land at home influence our decision. We accepted the vector for a GCA pickup and shot the approach.

Fortunately, we didn't get a student controller under instruction. We didn't flame out and we broke out just above mins. Back on deck, we reviewed our decision points and the circumstances that almost boxed us in.

Lessons Learned:

We should have realized the limitations and differences between CV and shore operations. As opportunities to fly dwindle with the occasional squeezes on OPTAR, we needed to temper the desire to fly and get the "X" with deviations from standard operating procedures and good judgment.

We should have resisted mental timesharing with personal business in the cockpit and focused on the flight 100 percent. Life is simpler on the boat.

NOTES:

F-14A + FOG = WORMS

F-14A TOMCAT, STRIKE FIGHTER SQUADRON ONE ZERO THREE (VFA-103) - JOLLY ROGERS

Lt. Owen G. Godfrey, March 1991

We were supposed to provide radar targets and data-link-systems checks for the ship. The warning area had been clobbered all day with low ceilings and layers up to 30,000 feet, all thanks to an occluded front. By late afternoon, the front had moved well out to sea, leaving behind a few scattered clouds. A quick check of the weather vision confirmed the clearing skies and improving conditions that we saw from our ready room windows.

We launched on time, Switched to strike and began drilling max-conserve circles around the boat. We ranged from 40 to 100 miles away from the coast at altitudes between 10,000 and 20,000 feet. During the two hours of systems checks, I monitored the fuel quantity to compare the actual consumption with the max-conserve fuel flow I had set on the LCD fuel-flow gauge. The F-14A(Plus) is notorious for burning more per hour than what the gauge shows. According to my calculations, we would have 5,000 pounds remaining at 2100. Since we could see the field from 50 miles, we had no qualms about sticking around until the end of our time block.

Our final vector positioned us 100 miles east of the field with a fuel state of 5,000 pounds. We called approach and started a max-range descent from 20,000 feet. By the time we had levelled off at 1,500 feet, we were feet dry, about 20 miles from the field. We were vectored to an ACLS Mode 2 to runway 5R. As we dirtied up, my RIO noticed what he described as "all those interesting patches of fog on the ground." We could still see the field as we set up on final. The field's ACLS went down right after lock-on and the controller told us to make a visual approach.

At 1,000 feet and 2.5 miles, we started flying in and out of a very thin layer. The extended centerline lights were visible throughout the approach but we still couldn't see the lens at One mile. We levelled off at 300 feet until we picked up a high ball at about three-quarters of a mile.

We were cleared for a touch-and-go, after which we switched to the tower's frequency for clearance downwind.

The tower cleared us to a right downwind because of FCLPs on 5L. Abeam the field, we noticed that the runway's extended center-line lights and the approach end were getting harder to see. Resorting to FCLP mentality, I flew the standard numbers. During the approach turn I could make out the extended centerline lights and, occasionally, portions of the threshold along with the lens. As I rolled onto final, all the visual cues disappeared and I realized that we were being swallowed up by a fog bank racing in from the southwest.

Instinctively, I levelled the aircraft with stick, but not enough power. I transitioned to an IFR scan and saw 200 feet on the altimeter, along with a 700-fpm descent and 18 units on the AOA gauge. I added power to climb out as I picked up the lens with a red ball. I told my RIO that I was going to land long and that I had the runway in sight. We touched down and rolled out to a safe stop.

As we taxied back to our line, we told the tower that 5R was IFR. Then we watched the fog bank roll in.

The FCLP birds were now making full-stop landings as the fog rolled 4,000 feet further down the runway, to the approach end of

5L. In a few minutes, the field was completely fogged in, down to zero-zero. My fuel gauge indicated 3.2 and the past events started to dawn on me. We missed having our flight turn into a can of worms by a very small margin, definitely a case of being lucky rather than good.

As I discovered the next day, weather had predicted possible fog down to zero-zero. In my confidence that the weather was going to improve all night, my attention had wandered during that part of the brief.

Lessons Learned:

If we had not landed when we did, we would not have been prepared to divert to any other field. We had not updated our weather and had no idea what the present or forecast conditions were.

It just goes to show you that just because something looks and smells good doesn't always mean it will be good.

NOTES:

TOO HOT TO HANDLE

F-5N TIGERSHARK,FIGHTER SQUADRON COMPOSITE ONE ONE ONE (VFC-111) - SUN DOWNERS

LCDR Derek Ashlock, Reported 2016

As a seasoned aviator, during Operation Desert Storm I had my fair share of emergencies. From losing an engine and performing a single-engine approach at the boat several times, to losing a leading edge flap inflight, I have an extensive experience dealing with situations outside the norm. Recently I encountered an event that quickly progressed from bad to worse.

I was leading a light division out of Key West (consisting of me in an F-5N and two Hawker Hunters on the 7 a.m. SFARP launch to act as red air strikers. Taking off from RW 32, power-up and wipe-out were normal and the ECS flow felt normal as did the temperature.

After a normal acceleration and takeoff —promptly as the gear came up and locked— and upon turning to our assigned heading, the ECS went past what I would consider normal full flow.

With the amount and velocity of the air coming out of the diffusers, I couldn't hear the radios. It was even more concerning that the temperature was something akin to a blowtorch and as if one wasn't enough, I immediately knew the combination of both was a serious situation. Initially trying to deflect the air blast coming from the right diffuser, the air was so hot that I could not hold my gloved hand over the airflow.

The outer control rings that meter airflow on the left canopy were literally too hot to touch so I could not turn them down or off, let alone divert their direction. I was amazed that flames were not accompanying the extraordinarily high temperature.

Mental note No. 1, "Golly, this is more serious than just hot air..."

Climbing through 1,500 feet armed with only my system knowledge because there is no procedure for this in NATOPS, I manually selected man cold to remove the auto temperature logic from the system. Knowing full well the advertised time required to effect change could be north of a minute, I gave it its due effort as much as I was able. After holding the toggle for 10 or 15 seconds with no change to flow or temperature, the heat building up in the cockpit was rapidly approaching unbearable. I abandoned this step and proceeded to my next course of action.

Mental note No. 2, "If RAM/DUMP doesn't work quickly, I'm going to have to jettison the canopy very, very soon..."

After reducing power, levelling at 2,500 feet and selecting RAM/DUMP on the pressurization switch, the amount and velocity of air coming through the system began to reduce but the temperature remained extremely hot. I could now hear the radio and I asked my Hawker Hunter wingman to back me up with my thought process as he was also qualified in the F-5N. He came back immediately with the same procedures I already had completed and that I was not trailing smoke or on fire. It was reassuring that I had acted properly and hadn't caused this myself or, even worse, forgot some simple step along the way. As mentioned before, there is no procedure in the F-5 NATOPS about runaway cockpit airflow/temperature.

With the airflow reduced and the temperature still hot but bearable, I passed the lead to the Hawker Hunter to press to the area and complete the red air presentation while I declared an emergency and coordinated my return to base with approach. I then spoke to my squadron ODO on AUX frequency who was brand new and on his first time on the desk. Confirming there was nothing in NATOPS to aid in my situation, I told him my game plan and then returned my attention to tower to alert them of my situation. I informed them of my problem and that I had it under control and would adjust my gross weight 5 miles south of the field. As the Tiger does not have a fuel dump system, I did a few afterburner 360s and landed with a 4.0 on the fuel on a 7,000 foot runway without issues.

Post-flight maintenance inspection discovered the bleed air regulator valve had failed to fully open, so full bleed air was coming into the cockpit directly from the engine. The extreme temperature of several hundred degrees and overwhelming velocity ultimately made sense.

Lessons Learned:

First, I have had my fair share of emergencies, but haven't had an emergency ramp up as fast to a near desperation level (consideration of jettisoning the canopy) in a matter of seconds before. The amount of airflow and heat was beyond my imagination. With no NATOPS procedures, only system knowledge that the RAM/DUMP switch would cease engine airflow to the cockpit and evacuate the extremely hot air aided me in handling this unique (to the F-5), situation.

Second, CRM was my friend. From communicating with my wingman for procedural backup and a visual inspection, to engaging our ODO to dig into NATOPS, to being directive with tower about my game plan, good crew resource management was a key factor in resolving this emergency in a safe, timely and efficient manner.

Lastly, with the historically volatile weather in the Florida Keys, I caught a break with basic VFR conditions. Had the weather been less than optimum, the attention that was required in the cockpit to battle the extreme heat could have led to disastrous results.

Often, as naval aviators we launch in less than ideal weather conditions, hardly pausing at the thought that bad things could happen let alone happen in a rapid manner. I have run the scenario through my head in bad weather or at night, and am thankful to have had this emergency during daylight and VFR conditions.

NOTES:

WHY ARE THOSE PEOPLE POINTING AT US?

SH-3D SEA KING, HELICOPTER COMBAT SUPPORT SQUADRON SIXTEEN (HC-16) - BULLFROGS

LCdr. C.W. Laingen, April 1996

When I found out that my first squadron assignment as a station pilot meant flying the SH-3D Sea King, I realized I'd have to re-learn the gear-down item in the landing checklist. I had been flying an aircraft with skids in flight school.

The first six months in the squadron passed, and I became a HAC. The aircraft's landing gear was just one of the many items that became second nature during those six months. One sunny afternoon, my SAR crew and I discovered that nothing was second nature.

Our flight took us along the coast, VFR, on the Fourth of July weekend. We were an airborne-SAR asset for the special events at the beaches, and we were primed for a rescue, especially since no one in the crew had ever made a real one.

As we watched the traffic along the two-lane beach highway from 500 feet, a light truck crossed the centerline and slammed head-on into an oncoming car, flipping the car and throwing it into the dunes. We watched the mishap in what seemed to be slow motion.

We reacted quickly. The HAC said, "I'm taking her down."

The statement made sense, and we prepared to land on the highway only seconds after the accident. As we were passing through 40 feet on the RADALT, the first crewman mentioned getting out to render assistance. I confirmed from the left seat that the cars were stopping in both directions to let us land – probably from fear of being sandblasted by the rotor wash. Everything seemed so natural, like the workings of a well-trained SAR crew that had flown together enough times to have no need to state the obvious.

However, as we passed 20 feet, my head came up out of the cockpit, and I suddenly had an uneasy feeling. I saw several people alongside the road pointing at the underside of the aircraft, but nothing clicked inside my head. I came back inside and quickly scanned the instrument panel. Something drew my gaze to the gear indicators, where I stared at two "UP" flags. I threw the gear handle down as I continued to stare at the indicators. Two barber poles indicating gear down bounced into the windows, and I simply said, "Gear down," to the HAC just as the aircraft touched the pavement.

Although it must have looked impressive, and planned, to the beachgoers who witnessed our landing, our debrief was anything but impressive.

Lessons Learned:

Not only was our potential rescue victim unhurt, our entire crew was embarrassed that we had not reacted properly. First, our preflight brief was clear that we would discuss any rescue before we tried it, no matter how short the discussion would be. Instead, we assumed that the situation could progress without words; our experience would back us up.

Second, I didn't listen to that inner voice that told me something was wrong 20 feet and seconds before landing. I should have stopped us at 20 feet to figure out what was bothering me.

NOTES:

CHAPTER 3

TOP GUN: MAVERICK

Lessons from TOPGUN Aircraft
featured in the movie, Top Gun: Maverick

"If you wish to have an eventful, exciting flight, don't prepare for it, don't brief situations and responsibilities, and don't plan on things changing on you... But for those of us who prefer to keep things boring and uneventful, I recommend that you fly like you train, expect the unexpected, and have a backup plan."

Lt. Trever Garabedian-Prophet
U.S. Navy

FEATURED AIRCRAFT

The following stories and lessons are from the actual aircraft, and variations of the aircraft, featured in the movie, *Top Gun: Maverick*.

Boeing F/A-18E Super Hornet

Designed and initially produced by McDonnell Douglas, the Super Hornet first flew in 1995. They are a twin-engine, carrier-capable, multirole fighter aircraft variants based on the McDonnell Douglas F/A-18 Hornet. 1997 saw the merger of McDonnell Douglas and Boeing. The Super Hornet entered fleet service with the United States Navy in 1999, replacing the Grumman F-14 Tomcat, which was retired in 2006. The Super Hornet's empty weight is around 11,000 lb (5,000 kg) less than that of the F-14 Tomcat which it replaced, not quite matching, the F-14's payload and range.

North American P-51 Mustang

North American Aviation (NAA) P-51 Mustang is a long-range, single-seat fighter and fighter-bomber used during World War II and the Korean War. The U.S. Air Forces, Flight Test Engineering, assessed the Mustang B stating:

"The rate of climb is good and the high speed in level flight is exceptionally good at all altitudes, from sea level to 40,000 feet. The airplane is very manoeuvrable with good controllability at indicated speeds up to 400 MPH. The stability about all axes is good and the rate of roll is excellent; however, the radius of turn is fairly large for a fighter."

TIME FOR THE CHAMBER

F/A-18E SUPER HORNET, STRIKE FIGHTER SQUADRON ONE NINE FIVE (VFA-195) - DAMBUSTERS

Lt. Michael Huntsman, December 2011

The day before a five day liberty port, I was scheduled for a good-deal day launch and a pinky night recovery to maintain currency. The plan was to launch, hit the tanker, execute 2 v 2 tactical intercepts, get a night trap and eat a slider at midrats.

My lead had received his gas from the tanker and was heading toward our briefed combat-air-patrol (CAP) point. I should have known things weren't going to go well when I had to join-up on my tanker in the clouds. I took 2,000 pounds from the tanker and got comfortably above my fuel ladder. When I got outside 10 miles from the carrier, I started a military-power climb toward our CAP. The weather was solid up to 21,000 feet, so I was instruments only until on top of the clouds.

Once on top, I transitioned to an outside scan and continued to climb. While still at military power and at about 28,000 feet, the environmental control system (ECS) surged. My ears popped, and I had trouble breathing. I can't fully recount all that transpired, but I do remember feeling lightheaded and disoriented. This feeling lasted for about 10 seconds, and then normal oxygen and ECS flow resumed. Still climbing at military power, the surging happened again about 30 seconds later, and I again felt lightheaded and dizzy. This time the feeling remained even after the flow became normal. I could only focus on one thing: aviate.

My lead called, "Fenced in," and I echoed that call while the ECS surged one more time. Then lead made the call to check in on the primary frequency, and I replied, "Stand by." I remember wanting to tell lead that I was hypoxic, but because of my confusion, I couldn't figure out how to make the call.

I transitioned to brain-stem power and executed the immediate action steps for Hypoxia/Low Mask Flow/No Mask Flow. I selected emergency oxygen and secured my OBOGS. I started a gentle descent, and for the first time since the ECS surging began, scanned my cabin altitude. It read 10,000 feet, which is within limits for 30,000 feet.

I told lead that I felt hypoxic. He suspected something was wrong, and although I did not realize it at the time, he had begun to join on me. He told me to select emergency oxygen. I said that I had done this step and had secured the OBOGS. He directed me to increase my rate of descent, and continue to below 10,000 feet cabin altitude. Because of poor weather below 21,000 feet, we decided to level off at 22,000 feet, where the cabin altitude read 8,000 feet. I secured the emergency oxygen and took off my mask. After about 10 minutes I began to feel normal. I was certain that I was no longer hypoxic, but overall felt about 80 percent.

We opened the pocket checklist (PCL) and reviewed the checklist for hypoxia while using the auxiliary radio. We discussed my condition and decided I would keep the navigation lead to avoid having to fly formation through the clouds while descending to marshal. We switched radio frequencies to talk to the squadron representative and get help from a third party back on the boat. I had the option to recover aboard the carrier or divert about 100 miles to NAF Atsugi. After some discussion, I insisted that I felt good enough to recover on the ship.

I began a slow descent to my holding altitude of 8,000 feet and again pulled the emergency oxygen. I started heading to the wrong marshal radial, and with help from my flight lead, got pointed in the right direction. I also put down my arresting hook, which I had forgotten to do. Because of my obvious confusion, I thoroughly reviewed my approach checklist. I again removed my mask and reseated the emergency oxygen.

I used the squadron-representative frequency to speak directly to my skipper, and he queried me about my physical state. I told him that I felt fine but was a little tired. He made the decision for me to land on the ship. This would give me the help of the ship's controllers and the landing-signal officers (LSOs), plus I wouldn't have to climb back up to a high altitude for the divert.

If I had diverted to Atsugi, I would have only had my flight lead to assist me and would have missed a delicious slider at midrats. Besides, if I was all jacked up on the approach, I could be waved off and still have had sufficient fuel to divert.

I commenced the approach on time. As soon as I was established on the final bearing at 1,200 feet, I latched up the auto pilot and again pulled the green ring. To my dismay, I realized that I hadn't fully seated the handle when securing the emergency oxygen and the O2 was depleted.

I wasn't receiving ACLS or ILS, which meant that I had to really concentrate on the approach. I started descending early, but just inside three miles, I began to receive ILS and realized I was low. I corrected the low position while flying the approach with my mask off.

With the mask hanging by the bayonet fitting, I called, "Hornet, ball" at three-quarters of a mile. I remember a power call or two from paddles and then a nice settle into the one wire.

After taxi, shutdown and post-flight paperwork — all done on muscle memory – I found myself standing in the ready room a little confused, feeling very tired and sluggish. The SDO mentioned that I needed to go to medical. "Where's medical?" I asked.

My flight lead escorted me to medical. The flight surgeon met me, assessed my state, and called the diving medical officer at Naval Base Yokosuka to relay my symptoms. With the possibility of decompression sickness, the ship's senior medical officer initiated a medevac.

With IV inserted and an oxygen mask on, I was put in a wheel chair and taken to the flight deck via the ordnance elevator. I must have been a sight to see, holding an IV in one hand and my O2 bottle in the other. Up on the flight deck and ready for the helicopter ride, someone threw a horse collar around my neck and put a cranial on my head; now I felt safe. I had a 20-minute helo flight, followed by an ambulance ride. After the diving medical officer examined me, I had to get in the recompression chamber right away. I spent five hours there and wasn't even allowed to sleep. I was diagnosed with Type II decompression sickness and hypoxia.

After thinking over and over again about this experience, I am convinced that my recent training in the reduced oxygen breathing device (ROBD) helped me recognize the symptoms of hypoxia and complete the appropriate emergency procedures. Great crew resource management (CRM), especially with my flight lead and squadron representative, was instrumental in helping me recover aboard the carrier. The doctors on the ship and at Yokosuka made an outstanding decision to medevac me, which allowed timely treatment for decompression sickness.

Lessons Learned:

A big lesson learned was that I should have remained on emergency oxygen until the symptoms of hypoxia had gone away (per the PCL). I should have coordinated to have medical personnel meet me at the jet to immediately take me to medical. Finally, I should have put in a to-go order for that slider.

I was fortunate to have recovered the aircraft and to have avoided serious medical issues from decompression sickness. I also beat the rest of the air wing back to Atsugi by about two hours.

NOTES:

WHERE'S THE GREEN RING?

F/A-18E SUPER HORNET, STRIKE FIGHTER SQUADRON THIRTY SEVEN (VFA-37) - RAGIN' BULLS

Lt. Zachary Matthews, December 2011

As much as I've enjoyed reading *Approach* stories over the last few years, my goal was to never write for this publication. My hope in drafting this article is that other aviators might learn a lesson from me and handle their time in the crucible differently.

This tale began in late March with a good deal cross-country with the XO and Ops O. Our Hornet light division took off from Gainesville and headed north. We spent the first half of the flight to Indianapolis dodging weather. As we crossed over Atlanta, we approached another cloud bank, and I began to move closer to my lead. I look inside my cockpit and briefly saw the two L/R BLEED warning lights illuminate. I heard Betty say, "Bleed air left, bleed air left." As quickly as they appeared, the red warning lights went out and the cockpit became much quieter. Then I saw three cautions on my left DDI: L BLEED OFF, R BLEED OFF and OBOGS DEGD (OBOGS - On-Board Oxygen Generation Systems).

I've only had several emergency-procedure (EP) sims. In my limited experience handling EPs in the simulator, the warnings came on and stayed on. I knew when a bleed-air leak occurred the bleed-air-leak detection (BALD) system should shut it down, however; I didn't know the warning lights would go out so suddenly once the leak was isolated. My OBOGS still appeared to be working despite the glaring caution that indicated otherwise.

I then reported to my lead, "I've got a problem here."

I told him that I had momentary bleed-air warning lights, but they had gone out. He then asked if I had inadvertently hit the fire test switch. "Well, maybe I did," I thought. Everything seemed normal, except for the cautions remaining on my DDI. It was entirely possible that I accidentally had hit the fire test switch, which would trigger the red warning lights and the aural tones, as well as shut off the bleed-air system. However, after the incident, I remembered that all the lights illuminate with the fire test switch and that Betty always starts with, "Engine fire left."

As I pondered the situation, like a deer staring in the headlights of a semi on I-95, I exhaled and suddenly couldn't breathe. When the OBOGS shut down with the rest of the ECS, residual air remained in the system. This air had just run out, and I had a perfectly sealed rubber mask on my face which prevented me from inhaling. The cabin pressure dumped as well, sending the contents of my sinuses down the back of my throat. My instinctual, and incorrect, response was to pop off my mask. While this was happening, I told lead exactly what I saw. He quickly and correctly surmised that I was dealing with an actual emergency.

He instructed me to "Pull the green ring."

I thought, "OK, the green ring, left side. Where's the green ring?" I could not find the green ring. I've strapped into a Hornet more than a hundred times (a lot, I know) and looked at that green ring every time. My problem was that I'd never actually put my hand on it in flight. I'm 6 feet 4 inches tall and my flight gear restricts my vision down into the cockpit. I couldn't see the green ring, so I couldn't pull it.

The effects of hypoxia were immediate and overwhelming. I was acutely aware that my mental faculties were quickly fading. I couldn't find the green ring where I expected it to be, and in my state of confusion, I somehow regressed back to my FRS days where some of the older jets have the green ring on the inside of the ejection seat. I was literally lifting up the seat cushion looking for it. I was panicking. I could feel my mind slipping away from me, all while trying to fly form in the clouds. I had enough useful consciousness to know that if I didn't find the ring within the next five-seconds I would need to do something else.

The definition of stupidity, or hypoxia, is to do the same thing over and over while expecting a different result. I was a prime example. I couldn't find the ring, so it was time to descend. I didn't discuss this decision with anyone. I made a unilateral decision as my lead and XO were trying to talk my eyes onto the green ring.

I heard, "Left thigh, left thigh!"

I then looked out to my left and saw the most beautiful, glorious thing I've ever seen: A big fat hole in the clouds to the west, complete with sunshine and blue skies. It was wonderful. "I'm going there," I thought.

"I'm descending," I said. I pushed the stick forward. My lead and the XO quickly become smaller.

As I began my descent, a radio call from lead cut through the hypoxia and rattled me into doing something useful.

I heard, "Left thigh, by the harness lock!"

I have used the harness lock before in flight; I knew where that was. I put my hand on it and went back an inch and, there it was: the green ring. I pulled it and felt the wonderful flow of oxygen. I put on my mask and the hypoxia symptoms immediately cleared. So, I had that going for me, which was nice.

"Is your mask on?" asked Dash 3.

"Yes, XO," I replied.

Everything was going to be OK, but the flight wasn't over, yet. I was in marginal VMC on top with the XO now on my wing, but my lead had continued on course. Remember, we were over Atlanta, one of the busiest aviation corridors in the country, and I had just rapidly descended 10,000 feet directly over the city. Our Atlanta Center controller apparently was a fan of the Navy and also happened to be Johnny on the spot with a suitable divert: Dobbins ARB. He immediately helped the emergency section (the XO and me) with a separate squawk and vectors to Dobbins. The XO and I read through the rest of the EP out of the PCL as we set up for our PAR.

The rest of the approach went well, and I touched down to a nice reception of fire trucks and ambulances. Say what you want about the Air Force, but the folks at Dobbins were wonderful hosts. Everyone from tower to the linemen were professional, and they did everything they could to help us out.

My squadron sent a maintenance detachment on Monday to fix the jet, so I could fly it back to Oceana. I found out that a $7.38 rubber boot connecting the ECS turbine to the bleed-air ducts exploded in the keel. The AME1 in charge of the maintenance detachment said he'd never seen one do that in more than 10 years of working on Hornets.

Lessons Learned:

What can you learn from my mistakes? The first step in the dual bleed-air-warning procedure is not to talk. The PCL states that you shall execute the boldface for warning lights "of any duration." Also, because the BALD system should immediately shut down the bleed-air system when it determines a leak, you may not see a warning light. The indications of a dual-bleed air warning may only be Betty, or just the associated BLEED OFF cautions and OBOGS DEGD.

This emergency really becomes three separate emergencies: dual bleed-off cautions, loss of cabin pressurization and low mask flow/no mask flow/hypoxia. The good news is that a common step that solves 95 percent of your problems: Emergency oxygen green ring – PULL.

Imagine if I immediately had pulled the green ring, as NATOPS instructs. "Lead, I had dual bleed-air warning lights. I've pulled the green ring, recommend descent to 10,000 feet." Done. Easy. Problem solved. Just land the airplane. Instead, I became hypoxic, almost losing a jet and my life.

Few emergency procedures in the Hornet need to be done right now. Pulling the green ring is one of them. We all know that we're supposed to, "Aviate, navigate, communicate," but you can't aviate if your brain is starved of oxygen. I communicated first. Big mistake.

You may see the green ring every time you get in the jet, but I strongly suggest that the next time you strap in, put your hand on it so you know where it is. Pull it if you want to. The great thing about the green ring is that you can reset it; it's not a one-way street. The Navy has plenty of gaseous oxygen to replace whatever you suck out of the seat pan; it really isn't a big deal to pull it if you don't need it. However, it is a big deal if you don't pull it when you should. That little ring is as important as the ejection handle. It's just as likely to save your life.

NOTES:

JUST ANOTHER AIRNAV

FA-18C HORNET, STRIKE FIGHTER SQUADRON ONE THIRTY ONE (VFA-131) - WILDCATS

LT Andrew Kiehaber, August 2014

It was a cloudy day in October when my wingman and I began our journey west, ferrying two FA-18Cs to the upcoming TOPGUN class. I had been told a week earlier to plan the trip and to prioritize military fields because of the current fiscal climate. After recently returning from two back-to-back cruises, an airways navigation (AIRNAV) across the United States seemed like an enjoyable way to get some much needed flight time, so I happily headed to our mission planning room and got to work.

Just like any AIRNAV, I began tracing out a route, finding diverts and prioritizing fields that were military and had arresting gear. After I had selected a route, I asked the maintenance officer (MO) what configuration we would have on our jets so I could calculate the drag index. We would be carrying a centerline fuel tank, an ATFLIR, one CATM-9X and two IMERs, which equated to a drag index of 150. I double-checked this calculation on the mission-planning computers and came up with a similar number. I then calculated the total fuel required for the first leg.

The first leg would be flown from NAS Oceana to NAS Meridian — 669 nautical miles, a reachable distance under normal conditions. I did not initially check the inflight winds during my preflight planning; however, I added 100 knots of wind from due west to make sure that we would be fine with a strong headwind component. Once all the preflight planning was complete, I determined that our first leg would be about 1.7 hours. We would land with 3,300 pounds of gas, well above daytime on deck standard-operating-procedure (SOP) fuel of 2,000 pounds. I showed my wingman the products; he concurred with the planning and was happy with the on-deck fuel.

The morning of the flight we briefed and looked at contingencies. We determined that the first leg would definitely be our most challenging because of the weather. Weather at NAS Oceana was broken at 800 feet. NAS Meridian was calling overcast at 500 feet because of a storm system moving slowly across the southeast U.S. Since the weather at our destination was less than visual flight rules (VFR) but greater than approach minimums, we needed a divert option with non-precision minimums plus 300 feet and 1 nm per OPNAVINST 3710. We had several diverts that were available, including Meridian International Airport (KMEI), Jackson-Evers International Airport (KJAN) and NAS Pensacola (KNPA). KNPA was actually a VFR divert if we needed to change our destination inflight. Surprisingly, both KMEI and KJAN showed considerably better weather than NAS Meridian, so we delayed our takeoff two hours and waited for weather to improve just to be sure that weather was developing as forecast.

After a two-hour delay, we decided the weather was satisfactory and we had three legal diverts. We knew that every last drop of gas was needed, so my wingman and I hot refuelled to top off the jets one last time before takeoff. Immediately upon takeoff, we experienced delays in climbing to our cruising altitude, but also noted that the wind was considerably stronger than forecasted. While the winds were roughly 80 knots at altitude, the direction was almost head on, not from the west as planned. As soon as we reached our altitude, I placed our destination under my active waypoint and brought up my flight-performance-advisory-screen (FPAS) page. The system calculated that I would be on deck with 2,800 pounds, roughly 500 pounds below my planned fuel on deck. While the fuel on deck was slightly lower, it was still above that mandated by SOP, and would provide enough gas to reach my two local diverts and hold for 20 minutes at max endurance. We continued as planned.

We proceeded along our route, constantly checking the weather using pilot-to-metro stations across the country to provide us with the most current weather in Meridian. We felt that the weather was staying the same with cloud layers right at TACAN minimums, and the visibility greater than 10 nm. I constantly checked my fuel page and rechecked my fuel on deck every 10 minutes, but much to my chagrin, fuel on deck continued to drop. Now, almost halfway between NAS Oceana and NAS Meridian, my fuel on deck read 2,200 pounds. While the changing FPAS-calculated fuel on deck concerned me, I still felt that I would be on deck above min fuel; however, quickly my divert options were starting to fade. While KNPA was a VFR divert, I would need to change my routing immediately to make it to Pensacola with 2,000 pounds of gas. After checking the weather one more time at our destination, we decided to continue along our route and proceed to Meridian.

We entered the Meridian terminal area, and again received an update on the weather - still no change. However, the PAR to the active runway was down. I checked fuel, and now my fuel on deck showed 1,800 pounds, a number that I was not happy with. After a quick decision, we declared minimum fuel with approach, and decided that we would take a PAR to the off-duty runway, one typically used for takeoff when NAS Meridian is using its northern runways.

Approach again passed the weather, and we determined that we should break out. If we didn't, and with our fuel at a lower state, we knew our divert options were quickly fading. At roughly 20 nm from

NAS Meridian, while flying formation in the clouds, I received the always jolting, FUEL LO caution. This caution comes on when either of the feed tanks is 800 pounds +/- 100, and normally comes on only when on deck. The caution made me feel uneasy, and I quickly started thinking about the impending approach and how would desperately need to break out.

At 15 miles from the field, approach instructed me to break off and head west. I would be the first aircraft to land because my wingman had slightly more fuel. As I broke off I checked my fuel level once again and saw that I was already at 1,900 pounds, expecting to burn almost 800 pounds in a normal approach. I then thought of every scenario I could manage: What I would do if I could not break out, where I would go, and how much time I truly had.

I knew that weather would certainly not be any better only 15 miles away at the KMEI, and KJAN was no longer a viable divert based on fuel. I made the choice to continue to an airfield that I knew had arresting gear and weather that was at TACAN minimums. I also knew that after this approach I couldn't divert anywhere else. As I commenced the approach, I did everything in my power to save fuel by flying my FPAS calculated, maximum-range Mach number until just inside the final approach fix. I would lower the landing gear at the fix.

After starting my descent in known instrument meteorological conditions (IMC), I started to break out sections of ground beneath me and what appeared to be the lowest layer of clouds. Eventually, at 400 feet, I broke out of the clouds and had 10 miles visibility. I had the runway in sight. I told my wingman that I had the field made, checked my gas one more time, and landed on the off duty runway with no issue. As I rolled out, I quickly cleared the runway for my wingman and checked my fuel - 1,500 pounds. My gas-saving measures had decreased my burn rate; however, I had landed below our SOP min fuel on deck. Both aircraft taxied to the line, shut down and we discussed what had happened.

Lessons Learned:

We quickly acknowledged that we hadn't had fun. We talked about the flight planning, and how the winds must have affected our numbers much more than expected, and how our decision to continue with the weather in IMC was not the right choice. While we were fortunate that both aircraft landed safely, it is yet another example of being out of gas and out of options.

While the Hornet is an amazing airplane, it still suffers the same pitfalls as any gas-powered vehicle and will cease to function without its precious JP-5. I have learned once again that you can press the weather or press fuel, but if you press both, you put yourself in a situation where you may have no options.

NOTES:

SITUATIONAL AWARENESS. WHEN YOU THINK YOU HAVE IT, BUT DON'T

F/A-18E SUPER HORNET, STRIKE FIGHTER SQUADRON FORTY ONE (VFA-41) - BLACK ACES

LT Jerome Teer and LTJG Joseph Izzo, October 2015

It was the last week of our three-week Air-to-Surface Strike Fighter Advanced Readiness Program (SFARP) at NAS Fallon. We were scheduled for a night Close Air Support (CAS) flight with a live GBU-16 in support of a joint terminal air controller (JTAC) qualification course. My WSO and I had flown five CAS events in the previous three weeks, and the mood was light after the brief. We were confident and ready to execute the mission.

We launched late (after our lead), proceeded to B-17 in the Fallon Range Training Complex and contacted the fires controller, Punisher 99. Reporting to Punisher 99, we were tactical administration complete, visual and in communication with our lead. We were cleared to switch to our JTAC, punisher 02, who cleared us into the same altitude block as our lead. Lead instructed us to hold cross circle on a hard altitude of 12,000 feet and give our full CAS check-in to Punisher 02.

Our lead had already expended his live GBU-16 and conducted a simulated attack, as we were setting up for our live GBU-16 attack.

Punisher 02 passed the game plan for the next attack: "Neutralize tanks in the open, one simulated GBU-16 from Fast Eagle 51, one GBU-16 from fast eagle 52, 90 second spacing, ground-based laser, Type 2 control, bomb on coordinate." Following the game plan, punisher 02 passed the 9-line and we began setting up for the attack.

I followed my normal habits. I confirmed we would make the TOT and calculated that we had a little over five minutes to execute the attack. I was in a position to set my spacing from lead, so I moved on to my next habit. I pulled out the imagery provided and plotted the coordinates on my chart to verify the target location within the B-17 range. My WSO began entering in the 9-line on the CAS page and plotting the coordinates on his chart as per normal tactical crew coordination (TCC) procedures. Those were the last procedures we executed correctly.

My WSO began his read back of the intended coordinates using the key words "from my system." The proper way to execute the read back of the target data is from the sub-level of the HSI display. Reading from this sub-level ensures the data is actually in the aircraft systems, and we have the proper target coordinates entered. However, my WSO incorrectly read back the data from the CAS page and not from the HSI sub-level. A benefit of a two-seat cockpit is having four eyes and two brains working a problem. This was not the case that night, because my execution of the procedures failed at this point as well.

I did not review the HSI sub level during his read back to QA our system setup per TCC. The target waypoint was never designated because neither one of us checked our aircraft system. In the four minutes remaining to our TOT, we failed to follow procedures, missing key checks that would have alerted us that our intended target was not designated situational awareness (SA).

Just prior to pushing and setting up for our attack, we looked at the advanced tactical forward looking infrared (ATFLIR) display to see where we were designated. The ATFLIR was in a narrow field of view, not allowing for a proper target area QA. We mistook what we saw for what we expected to see in our target area per the brief. Had we taken the time to do a proper QA by increasing the field of view, we would have noticed several key features that would have alerted us it was not our target assigned by the JTAC.

Most notably, the coordinates where the ATFLIR was designated were not the coordinates of the target passed in the 9-line. It was a bomb on coordinate attack, and my WSO had not moved the designation so the coordinates should have matched. As we continued our attack run, we ran through our air-to-surface checklist.

My WSO did his checks and reported he was "checks complete in the back, waiting for master arm, and TDC," which is standard for a two-seat crew. I ran through my checklist, placed my TDC to the HUD, and placed the Master Arm switch to ARM.

I reported, "Checks complete in the front, we are armed up." However, we were not checks complete, because neither one of us QA'd the designation. The HSI display would have shown us the wrong target designated, and after we reviewed our tapes, there was no doubt according to the ATFLIR display that we were not in the target area.

I allowed the SA display and my spacing to take all my focus. As we pressed for our attack, I didn't QA the designation on the ATFLIR, nor did I obtain positive identification (PID) of the target, which is required per training rules to release live ordnance. My WSO focused on not making an error in ordnance system set up and switchology so he, also, never looked at the ATFLIR display. Ten-seconds prior to release, having received a cleared hot, and I released our live GBU-16, thinking we had good SA. My WSO executed the appropriate JLASE communications, as I executed an offset to the right.

The bomb hit 1.5 miles short of the target, about 100 meters south of our echo point. For those familiar with the B-17 complex, 100 meters south of the runway apex is a part of the range where live GBU-16s are not authorized. I was looking outside after the release, again, never looking at the ATFLIR display.

The first indication I received that the bomb did not hit the intended target was when our lead asked the JTAC where the bomb impacted. I remember my first thought being, "What's he mean, 'where did the bomb hit?'"

Lessons Learned:

This first thought demonstrates the worst type of incorrect SA. My WSO and I thought our SA was high; however, the exact opposite was true. We allowed our SA "bubbles" to shrink, allowing the most important thing to fall outside our SA. Procedures and training rules are in place for this specific reason. Had we followed the procedures properly and abided by training rules, we could have caught the multiple errors we made in time to correct them. The bomb hit dirt, 1.5 miles away from any friendly forces or range personnel. That wasn't the case in the 2001 mishap in the Udairi Range. It has been difficult moving past the feelings of"what if?" I could not imagine the feelings of "what did I do?" which was definitely a possible outcome that night.

In the Super Hornet community every flight is a training flight. Even the benign airway navigation flights, we plan tactics to practice along the route. We train constantly for a reason. When the time comes that our buckets are full, hanging on to the stabs and trying to catch up, or we are low SA and don't realize it, it is our training and our adherence to procedures and training rules that will keep us and others safe.

NOTES:

WHICH WAY IS RIGHT?

F/A-18E SUPER HORNET , STRIKE FIGHTER SQUADRON TWO SEVEN (VFA-27) - ROYAL MACES

LCDR Michael Miller (former TOPGUN instructor), Dec 2015

As soon as I stepped on the flight deck, I could see the solid gray overcast and knew the weather was not ideal for my red air flight. My flight lead and I had attended a mass coordination brief an hour prior in which we were directed to simulate "seasoned and aggressive adversaries." Essentially, training restrictions had been removed, and we were authorized to execute aggressive, three-dimensional manoeuvring in order to arrive at a merge unobserved (thereby wreaking havoc upon the blue fighter formation).

However, given the look of the clouds, I doubted there was enough clear air to conduct a large air-to-air fight in the manner we desired, therefore favoring the fighters, in their mission, to attrite us.

My hopes improved as I climbed off the catapult. The cloud cover was widespread, but the overcast layer was higher than it looked from the flight deck. I completed my weapons checks for my particular red air simulation and joined my flight lead, a section lead under instruction who was only a few flights away from earning his section lead qualification. We proceeded to our cap and held below the weather at 14,000 feet and waited for the fighters to check in.

The fighters reported unworkable weather in the south and the bandits reported the same in the north. "Well, so much for this event," I thought glumly, quickly concluding there was no way to accomplish the training objectives for a large-force, air-to-air event.

The fighter lead reached the same conclusion. Over the primary frequency, he declared the event cancelled due to weather, and we all broke off into individual elements to pursue alternate missions. Normally, when assigned to conduct red air support, our squadron briefs 1v1 basic fighter manoeuvres (BFM) if there is fuel and airspace available.

Thinking there would be no way to execute BFM with the surrounding weather, my flight lead sighted a clear pocket of airspace about 10 miles in diameter and below a high overcast layer with a clearly defined horizon. Having briefed the requisite training rules as well as position, altitude, distance and speed (PADS) for our engagements, we suddenly became the recipients of a dedicated 1v1 BFM hop. I eagerly began adjusting my displays and recorders, preparing my cockpit for dynamic manoeuvring. I had no way of knowing that in a few minutes I would be roaring upward into the vertical, gripping the controls in sheer terror.

Our first engagement was benign and ended with us both arriving neutral on the deck. It was clear that neither of us were likely to gain a decisive positional advantage so we knocked off the fight.

The second engagement began much the same as the first. After a second neutral lateral left-to-left pass at approximately 9,000 feet, my flight lead elected to roll wings level and execute a pull into the vertical. For those not well-versed in FA-18 BFM doctrine, a pure vertical move can be decisive if the adversary can't or won't make a follow-on merge due to either lack of energy or lack of recognition.

However, if properly countered, as I was preparing to do, the lower aircraft can quickly turn the tables by using the effects of gravity to rapidly reverse out of the vertical following the upcoming low-to-high merge.

As a former TOPGUN instructor, I relished moments such as these where I had the opportunity to win a fight decisively and illustrate a fundamental learning point in terms of flow and decision making.

However, as I pulled up into the vertical, I witnessed something that was first unfamiliar... then outright terrifying. As my flight lead completed his over-the-top manoeuvre, I placed him just outside my right canopy bow. I was looking up at the top of his aircraft as his nose was pointing to my right, out of the vertical. I expected that he would ease his pull and extend a bit to my right in an attempt to flatten out our upcoming pass. However, I watched in horror as he increased his pull nose low in front of my flight path and I found myself staring up at the underside of his jet falling rapidly towards me.

Although my flight lead had not called "blind" on the radio, I knew immediately that he had likely lost sight of me as I could no longer see his canopy.

By pulling his nose down and across mine, we were now on a collision course with more than 400 knots closure. I distinctly remember thinking, "Oh my God, we're going to hit," as my stomach turned over with the flood of adrenaline into my system.

I could not think of anything to say on the radio to help him avoid my aircraft and simply tried to keep my flight path predictable. As we closed to within a few thousand feet, my flight lead finally gained enough airspeed to roll 180 degrees to the left and regain sight. Observing my slow roll to the left, he pushed his stick smoothly forward and right, opening up our flight paths to a 400-500-foot pass in the vertical.

My mouth was dry and it took me a few seconds post 3-9 line passage to finally make a "knock-it-off" call on the radio. We recovered aboard the aircraft carrier uneventfully.

OPNAV 3710 as well as the Joint Typewing Core SOP both provide clear and consistent training rules and procedures for flight path deconfliction. In the case of a head-on pass, fighters are directed to maintain the established trend. If no trend exists, give way to the right to make a left-to-left pass. If there is any doubt about the "established trend," fighters are instructed to transmit their own intentions.

In order to alleviate confusion between left and right when aircraft are upside down, the pass should be called "earth-stabilized." If two aircraft meet at the top of a loop it may look like a right-to-right pass to an inverted pilot but should be called left-to-left (God's eye view). If the pilot is disoriented, he should roll wings level. The final deconfliction measure applicable in our case states that forward-quarter radar-lock attempts shall not be attempted inside of 1.5 nm, which my flight lead later told me he was attempting to do when he crossed in front of my projected flight path.

At first glance, it would appear that my flight lead blatantly violated these training rules in rapid succession. It appeared to me that we had a right-to-right trend established which was not maintained. Specifically, his forward-quarter radar lock taken inside of 1.5 nm denied flight path deconfliction, resulting in a "blind lead turn," or an intentional manoeuvre to lose sight. However, upon review of our heads-up-display (HUD) footage, I was surprised to see how insidiously this situation developed in my flight lead's cockpit. While it was still a training rule violation, his jet clearly seemed to "fall" into this unsafe situation rather than being carelessly or over-aggressively placed there by pilot action.

He explained his intent was to achieve a radar lock at what he assessed to be approximately two nautical miles. However, he was slow and it took longer for his nose to track. His pitch control was so sluggish he overshot causing his predicted flight path to cross mine.

Lessons Learned:

This pass appeared to me right-to-right. However, in a steep merge, earth-stabilized "left" and "right" loose meaning. Traditional communication may not be effective. Care must be taken during BFM instruction to brief the characteristics of reduced nose authority when nose high or when pulling out of the vertical nose low. Expect sluggish pitch control and ensure deconfliction by keeping the other aircraft out of your HUD. Consistently safe vertical merges can be accomplished following these guidelines.

While we didn't learn as much on this hop as the fighters would have learned from the "seasoned and aggressive" game plan we had developed, we learned an important lesson about BFM. Air-to-air training is important to be ready for future conflicts. With proper teaching and effective briefing, we can safely train aggressively and realistically.

NOTES:

NOT THE IDEAL HAWAII VACATION
F/A-18E SUPER HORNET, STRIKE FIGHTER
SQUADRON EIGHT ONE (VFA-81) - SUNLINERS

Lt Jake Hawley, December 2015

Not more than two weeks into what would turn out to be a busy ten-month deployment in support of Operation Inherent Resolve (OIR), I found myself in a divert situation that would buy me a couple of days away from typical boat life in favor of the arduous living conditions of Hawaii. One evening, my flight lead and I launched from the deck of the USS Carl Vinson (CVN 70) to execute what was supposed to be a routine training flight in the waters off Hawaii.

Our mission was to practice the time-honored tradition of unguided air-to-surface roll-in attacks on the open ocean at night. In order to complete our training for the evening, we would first employ a pair of MK-58 marine location markers. We would use them as targets during multiple roll-in attacks with MK-76 light inert bombs. Rather than helping to preserve our night roll-in currency while keeping several of our readiness matrix blocks green, the markers and 76s would instead produce a basic NATOPS check for compound emergencies, a blown tire and a brake fire.

During the preflight brief, we spent a comfortable amount of time reviewing the local area, including the ins-and-outs of our divert airfields, the primary being Hickam Air Force Base in Honolulu, Hawaii. With all of this in mind, the brief, preflight, and launch all went off without a hitch. Once airborne, my flight lead and I quickly joined the flight and proceeded toward the working area. While en route we elected to complete as much tac admin as possible and initiated a "standard" G-warm. It only took about 4 G's and 90 degrees of turn before we were interrupted by the master caution light illuminating and the "engine right, engine right" audible warning tones. A quick "knock it off" call and a cursory scan of my cockpit revealed the master caution light to be illuminated. Further inspection revealed an R ENG caution as well as a full authority digital engine control (FADEC) advisory.

I quickly pulled the right engine throttle to idle and rolled the aircraft straight and level, I communicated my current predicament with my flight lead and requested that he join on me as I worked to scan the engine page. The jet was flying fine with no control issues at all; however, I quickly noticed that my R ENG had been commanded to idle by the FADEC. This meant that the FADEC sensed a problem with the right engine, took control of said engine, and locked the N2 RPM at a flight-idle setting.

My flight lead and I confirmed completion of the immediate-action items. I turned the flight back toward the ship and worked to contact the CATCC rep for assistance with the remainder of the checklist. As user-friendly as a single-seat, Lot 30 F/A18E can be, I still found that trying to read a checklist at night while continuing to aviate, navigate and communicate results in a full bucket and a greater risk of mis-interpretation of emergency procedures. In light of this, we contacted our CATCC rep who executed solid CRM and worked me through the checklist. He also had me check for engine responsiveness. Wherever I moved the throttle, the engine maintained a flight idle state with no response.

Based on the close proximity of a good divert and single-engine considerations at night, it must have been a no-brainer. I quickly got a divert and was on my way to Hawaii.

My flight lead planned to lead me into an approach to the open runway at Honolulu/Hickam. He then planned to execute a low approach and head back to the ship for a trap after I had made it safely on deck. We declared an emergency and put Hickam on the nose. I started adjusting fuel to arrive at an aircraft weight that was commensurate with a comfortable field landing and worked through my ship-to-shore checklist. I was feeling at ease with how things were working out and anticipated an easy landing and shutdown followed by a night in Hawaii prior to the rescue det arriving.

The approach went as advertised, and I made a gentle landing near the beginning of the approach end of the runway, taking full advantage of the 9000-foot roll out. On touchdown I felt a sense of relief and applied a normal brake pressure all the way to the end of the runway.

I didn't notice that my right engine maintained a flight idle N_2 RPM of 73 percent instead of reducing to a normal ground idle of just over 61 percent. The increased engine RPM required an increased amount of braking. The increased friction generated heat that I failed to recognize.

After clearing the runway, I was instructed by the tower controller to hold position and wait for the civilian emergency vehicles. It took approximately 5-10 minutes for the emergency crews to arrive. Following a walk around and visual inspection, they reported nothing unusual. I was soon cleared to continue taxiing to the hot cargo pad at Hickam Air Force Base, where Hickam Air Force emergency crews would meet me with the intent of de-arming the MK-76 and maritime markers once safely in the contained area. The taxi to the hot cargo area was approximately 9,000 feet and seemed normal.

As I pulled into the hot cargo pad, the emergency crew told me that my left tire had blown 100 feet before I stopped taxing.

I noticed a flash of light under the left wing as a fire started on my left brake assembly. The crew quickly directed a stream of AFFF on the fire and put it out within a few seconds.

Lessons Learned:

There are multiple learning points from this event. After landing rollout, during the subsequent hold-position evolution, a closer inspection of my engine parameters would have revealed a higher than normal N2 RPM.

This should in turn have raised a flag that increased levels of braking would be necessary, potentially causing additional heat generation from the brake assembly. Once clear of the runway, the best option would have been to secure the engine and coordinate a tow to the hot cargo area.

NATOPS doesn't cover every situation that aircrew may encounter. It is up to aircrew to build a solid understanding of aircraft systems and make educated decisions when compounded scenarios arise.

NOTES:

NO HYDS, NO PROBLEM

EA-18G GROWLER, ELECTRONIC ATTACK SQUADRON ONE THREE THREE (VAQ-133) - WIZARDS

LCDR Adam Green, March 2017

Flying on the first day out of port is typically avoided for a whole host of reasons. However, after many days of transit and upon completion of our first port call of deployment on the lovely island of Guam we were eager to get back into the air. My EWO and I were scheduled for a good-deal, daytime tactical intercept flight. It was a one-hour cycle and the weather was clear except for a thin cloud layer between 2,000 and 5,000 feet MSL.

While executing an abort manoeuvre during the first intercept, the aircraft was at about 9,000 feet MSL and approximately 450KIAS when we received a master caution with displayed HYD5000, HYD 2A and HYD 2B cautions. My first thought was, "This is why we don't fly the first day out of port". However, after processing the cautions we immediately called "knock it off" and brought the right throttle back to idle. I initiated a climb and slowed down while we broke out the pocket checklist (PCL) to start working through the problem.

After realizing that the left engine just became our new best friend, we started formulating a game plan for our recovery. Cyclic operations require a few added levels of coordination depending on the severity of the emergency. In the EA-18G Growler, the HYD 2A and 2B systems powers half of the flight controls and all of the systems needed for a normal landing (i.e., landing gear, nose wheel steering, and normal brakes). Due to the quickness with which we received both cautions (no reservoir level sensing (RLS) system indications) we suspected a blown hydraulic line, which meant we also lost our emergency braking and fuel probe extension system.

Once the dust settled from the initial indications, we had our wing man join on us for a visual inspection. Everything looked normal so we began flying a maximum endurance profile to the carrier to conserve fuel (at the time we had 11k, which was well above ladder) and started talking to the ship via J-Voice A to inform them of our emergency and to get our Pri-fly rep in the tower to start coordinating for recovery. This emergency was going to require us to emergency extend the landing gear with no way to raise it once it was down. The good news was that every aircraft carrier in the Navy comes equipped with arresting gear unlike some airfields, so braking wasn't going to be much of an issue. The bad news was that fuel quickly becomes an issue when the only option is executing a dirty bingo profile. Tanking with the landing gear down was not going to be an option due to the fact that our fuel probe extension and emergency extension relies on hydraulic fluid from the HYD 2B system (now empty). Fortunately for us, we were not operating blue water. The nearest divert (Andersen Air Force Base on Guam) was only about 80 miles away.

The tower representative coordinated with the Air Boss, informing him of the nature of our emergency, the requirement for a tow out of the wires, and our inability to raise the hook. Meanwhile, we verified all steps were completed from the PCL, informed the ship of our plan to come down last for a straight-in approach, ran the dirty bingo numbers, and passed that we would need to stay mid-range on the power in the wires until we were chocked.

Tower informed us that they would manually push us out of marshal and clear us to blow down our landing gear at the appropriate time, which enabled us to conserve as much fuel as possible. We flew a standard day straight-in with no issues.

Lessons Learned:

If I were to choose when to have a HYD 2A/2B failure I couldn't think of a better time. We had lots of fuel, decent weather and a divert airfield close by. The HYD emergency did not require us to shut down the right engine, so we were able to fly a normal approach. The discussion to have in your ready room is two-fold. First, what actions and coordination need to be performed in this situation and with whom? Second, what thought processes, crew resource management, and decision making need to occur in the cockpit with night time, blue water operations, or single engine considerations? Despite all of our coordination there was still confusion on the flight deck about why we were not at idle in the wires and not raising our hook. It only takes one broken link in this long chain of events to turn a well-executed emergency into a SIR.

NOTES:

AN UNCOMFORTABLE PLACE

F/A-18E SUPER HORNET, STRIKE FIGHTER SQUADRON ONE ONE THREE (VFA-113) - STINGERS

LT Kristi Hansen, March 2017

It was going to happen eventually. All good things come to an end, and my incredibly lucky run of avoiding display issues at the boat came to a screeching halt on a "pinky" cat shot two weeks into our composite training unit exercise (COMPTUEX).

The master caution went off as the jet started to fly away and the light in the gear handle accompanied with a continuous beeping tone immediately caught my attention. Worried that my gear had not come up, I tried to double check my airspeed to find that the airspeed box in the heads up display (HUD) was empty. Not entirely sure what was wrong at the time, I continued to climb until I was sure I was nowhere near the water. Passing 5,000 feet, the radar altimeter (RADALT) kicked off and I lost my altitude reference as well. Glad that I still had some horizon left, I called for assistance and started to cycle through my displays. I had an AIR DATA caution and an associated air data computer (ADC) MUX fail on the BIT page. My worst nightmare of a standby recovery at the boat was finally occurring and to make matters worse the marine layer was moving in and the moon was nowhere in sight.

According to NATOPS, the ADC receives inputs from numerous sources and calculates accurate air data and magnetic headings. Information is supplied to the mission computers, the altitude reporting function of the IFF, engine controls, environmental control system, landing gear warning, and the fuel pressurization and vent system. From a piloting standpoint, the loss of airspeed and barometric (BARO) altitude is disconcerting but to make matters worse, the velocity vector may become inaccurate after approximately 10 minutes and the procedures call for the ATT switch to be placed in standby (STBY). For all of us who have become velocity vector cripples, this is a major degradation of one's scan within the cockpit. The landing signals officer (LSO) sight picture is affected as well since the outside AOA indexers do not function.

I was directed to use ground speed as an airspeed reference until I could get my gear down and use the "E" bracket for AOA control. The decision was made for me to return with the current recovery, so I had plenty of gas to fly around dirty. As my hopes of being mercifully diverted to North Island dwindled, I requested that a tanker join on me prior to descending through what had become a black abyss. Standby instruments function normally with an ADC failure, but flying steam gauges as my sole altitude reference until 5,000 feet was not my idea of a good time.

With the tanker on my wing, I found it easier to retain the lead vice flying form. It gave me a chance to get used to the standby sight picture on the HUD and take things at my own speed. My TACAN was intermittent and my tanker escort did an outstanding job of driving me around and backing me up on my altitude and rate of decent. He told approach that he would set me up on the straight in and that they could start directing us once we were lined up. Thankfully, the ILS was still functioning which significantly enhanced my reference points. The ILS and my wingman dropped me off on a decent start and Paddles was able to talk me into the wires.

Finally on deck, I was very thankful for the crew coordination that helped me get there safely. I was able to get help in quickly sorting out functioning reference points for airspeed and altitude. My wingman assisted in my descent and line up, and Paddles put the finishing touches on a flight that I would rather never repeat.

Lessons Learned:

Although I had practiced standby approaches at the field, I was not expecting the lack of VSI in the HUD and the inability to use auto throttles that came with a full ADC failure. In addition, this failure reiterated the importance of referencing 10 degrees of pitch attitude with the waterline symbol coming off of the cat. If my cat shot had occurred just a couple of minutes later I would have launched without a visible horizon and with a questionable velocity vector. Not a comfortable place to be.

My next set of carrier qualification workups will definitely incorporate ADC failures in the simulator. Up to this point, I have always just selected STBY on the HUD to simulate a standby approach. Unfortunately, as mentioned above, this does not completely imitate the totality of systems lost. Practice, a knowledgeable representative and some help from paddles is essential in turning a bad night into an earned meal at midrats.

NOTES:

TAKE IT AROUND!

F/A-18E SUPER HORNET, UNIT WITHHELD

LT Loren Bluhm, March 2017

On July 1, 2014, a beautiful VMC day, our flight out of Naval Air Station (NAS) Lemoore quickly turned into a flight to remember. Within ten minutes of takeoff, the flight was interrupted by the failure of the left generator in my F/A-18E Super Hornet aircraft indicated by a L GEN caution. Utilizing good crew resource management (CRM), I communicated with the squadron duty officer (SDO) on the base radio frequency and completed all procedures using my NATOPS pocket checklist. I decided to return to base and land the aircraft. After coordinating with approach control and tower, I made my way back to NAS Lemoore and into the day landing pattern. After entering the pattern, I completed my landing checklist and received clearance to land.

No malfunctions were apparent in the cockpit; gear was down and locked with flaps set to full. As soon as I touched down I noticed a light in the gear handle, a flashing left main gear light, and the audible gear tone. The jet had no problems with handling as I continued down the center of the runway. My first thought was that I had some sort of sensor failure because I had no loss of directional control with the aircraft. I began to brake; as soon as the aircraft began to slow it swerved aggressively to the left, and I departed the runway at speeds near 80 knots. I reached for the ejection handle, pulled, and the simulator immediately froze. "It's on freeze, you are cleared to get out," my simulator instructor said. Not properly reacting to indications and completing the necessary NATOPS boldface procedure was an easy lesson to learn that day with no real consequences. A disappointed sim instructor was the worst thing I faced and I lived to finish the Fleet Replacement Squadron.

On March 16, 2017, a terribly dark night flight out of NAS Fallon, quickly brought back the memory of my disappointed sim instructor. The mission was a division, night self-escort strike during the Strike Fighter Advanced Readiness Program (SFARP) detachment that my squadron was conducting as part of our biennial training requirement. Start-up, taxi, and takeoff were uneventful and no mechanical issues were noted. The mission went mostly as planned and ended in mission success. The division lead fenced out the flight, and my section lead and I detached to return to base as a section. We followed the vectors given to us from approach control, soon had the field in sight, and we then proceeded to the initial for pattern entry. After entering the pattern, I completed my landing checklist and received clearance to land. No malfunctions were apparent in the cockpit; my gear was down and locked and flaps set to full. As soon as I touched down I noticed a light in the gear handle, a flashing left main gear light, and the audible gear tone.

My first thought was that I had some sort of sensor failure because I had no loss of directional control with the aircraft. At that moment, my disappointed sim instructor's voice echoed in my head and reminded me to execute the NATOPS boldface procedures and go around. As I selected max afterburner and began to accelerate, I felt a slight pull to the left as my aircraft began to fly again. As soon as I was airborne, all indications disappeared and my cockpit was again quiet with no tones. I coordinated with the tower for an altitude sanctuary, levelled off, and began to coordinate with the SDO on the base radio. I did not change my aircraft configuration since I did not know what failure I had (if any).

After executing good CRM with the SDO, I completed all procedures using my NATOPS pocket checklist. I then began to coordinate a fly in arrestment. Tower cleared me for a short-field arrestment on the off-duty runway because they did not want me to foul the main runway in use. As I began to set up for the fly in arrestment, I soon realized I could not see where the arresting gear wire was located. I could not see the arresting gear location lights either, and I had no time to get a landing signal officer (LSO) on station for a "paddles" talk-down into the runway arresting gear. The runway did have an Improved Fresnel Lens Optical Landing System (IFLOLS) providing glideslope reference, so I elected to fly a center ball (or as close to glideslope as I could) to touchdown. I was almost certain the "meat ball" would probably drive me short of a fly in arrestment, however, I was confident that I would have the ability to maintain directional control until arrestment based on aircraft performance during my first landing attempt.

As soon as I touched down, I put the throttles at idle. Again, the light in the gear handle, the flashing left main gear light, and the audible gear tone appeared. Once again, my jet tracked straight and I had no directional control issues. I rolled about 300 feet into the arresting gear and I immediately knew I had a good trap. The aircraft began to decelerate, and I felt a hard pull to the left. I countered the pull by applying right rudder to use the nose wheel steering and it only helped slightly. I came to a stop in the center of the runway and I had about a 30 degree left heading difference when compared to the runway. The crash crew made their way to my jet and chocked the wheels.

I waited a few minutes for maintenance personnel to tow my aircraft back to the line. When they arrived they immediately signalled to me they would not be able to tow the aircraft without more equipment.

I shut the aircraft down and gave them custody of the jet. I climbed out of the jet, down the ladder and saw the left main landing gear cocked with a thirty-degree inward cant angle. The tire itself looked to be made of fabric, as it no longer possessed rubber. How the tire did not explode or come apart I do not know. The planing link had failed, as it was just dangling from one end. Adrenaline shot into my veins at that moment. There is no doubt in my mind that my jet would have departed the runway had I not executed the proper emergency procedure.

Lessons Learned:

The first lesson I learned that night is the same lesson I learned as an FRS student three years prior - always react and treat indications from the aircraft as if they are a worst-case scenario. I could have trapped with no planing link failure that night, but the potential for negative consequences from not executing the proper procedure were extremely high. I continually try to remind myself that traps are free, even if it is just precautionary. And even though they may not be "completely" free, they are much less costly than the loss of a jet or worse, loss of life. The second lesson I learned is that we are the best-trained pilots in the world.

<u>NOTES:</u>

WHAT ELSE COULD GO WRONG?

F/A-18E SUPER HORNET, STRIKE FIGHTER SQUADRON ONE THREE SEVEN (VFA-137) - KESTRELS

LT Jeff Findlay, September 2017

Just when I thought nothing else could go wrong one day, I looked up and saw a face full of EA-18G. I'm fortunate to be here to tell my story. However, every thought I have of September 14, 2017 comes with a feeling of queasiness, and I wait for the day I won't be affected by this story or others like it.

That day marked my third week of Air Wing Fallon and large force strikes (LFSs) on the Fallon Range Training Complex (FRTC). LFS planning is a multi-day evolution. The strike's mission planning factors are given to the mission commander (MC) a couple of days prior, and the MC receives briefs from intelligence officers, targeteers, and weather forecasters. The load plan and associated aircrew are provided the day prior. On this particular event, CAG was briefed on the plan the morning of, the final details were hashed out in mission planning throughout the morning, and the event itself was executed in the afternoon.

I was a senior pilot finishing up my department head tour at VFA-137 attached to CVW-2, and was awaiting transfer to my next command. On this particular day, mission planning started at 0830, and my job was to carry and employ an anti-radiation missile (ARM). By no means is this a glamorous job, but I certainly didn't want to be the one to mess things up. Failure could cause the strike package to be threatened and shot at by surface-to-air missile systems.

My aircraft was loaded with three ARM captive air training missiles (CATMs) and my portion of mission planning was fairly easy, but time-consuming, due to my relative inexperience with the weapon. Although the air wing and I were not as proficient as we would have liked based on operational and maintenance constraints, the plan for the strike was well within our capabilities. For my part, I would keep visual contact with those entities I was supposed to protect and employ weapons as required. The EA-18G Growlers held command of the suppression of enemy air defense (SEAD) package and our division, while I was in charge of my section of FA-18Es.

Simple, right? I thought, "Easy day."

After the mass and element briefs, my wingman and I headed to our ready room confident we knew the game plan, which included our section owning 27,000 feet in the rendezvous stack and the knowledge of where everyone else was going to be in that stack. Our focus then shifted to getting mentally ready, rewarding ourselves with a sandwich, loading mission cards, and getting dressed in order to make it to the jets for a timely start. However, after walking back to the hangar and looking at dark skies, we should have guessed our plan was about to change.

Once in the ready room, we were told by the squadron duty officer we were in thunderstorm condition 1 (T-1). T-1 went until 1530, which was our walk time. During T-1, NAS Fallon prohibits fuelling, the uploading and downloading of ordnance, and personnel on aircraft. In other words, the aircraft sat idle from the time T-1 was called until it was lifted, around an hour total. My aircraft had its ordnance loaded and was fuelled prior to T-1, so I walked at the normal time. However, the other four aircraft in my squadron were still not prepared for the training mission, and ultimately required a lot of maintenance manpower to get back the hour lost to weather.

I started up my jet in accordance with NATOPS, and the "Ordies" armed my ARM CATMs. Hoping to get out of the line quickly to allow our maintenance personnel to concentrate on my peers' aircraft, I taxied out in a relatively short time. However, as I finished powering up my systems, I noticed one of my ARM missiles was not functioning properly and had to taxi back in. My wingman had yet to even start up.

As I began to troubleshoot, I heard it questioned over our base frequency if the mission time would be shifted (rolex) or canceled due to the time. The answer was to continue to move forward, but without delineating a new timeline. This is where I could have first helped the situation, and recommended a formal rolex. Since LFSs are scripted and executed based on a timeline, knowing the timetable you are working with is critical to keeping everyone on the same page. I've heard this done many times in my prior experience, but I failed to make the recommendation on this event. Instead, I concentrated on getting my jet into a flying condition, picking up my wingman, and getting airborne. Allowing someone else to make the call or take action is known as diffusion of responsibility. We know it plainly as, "That's his job, not mine." I was 100 percent guilty of it here, but wait and read on ... it only gets worse.

After some troubleshooting on deck, which included cycling my mission computers, I noticed my once "tight" Link-16 information was now corrupt. From experience, I knew Link-16 wouldn't come back unless I did a cold shutdown, aka "control-alt-delete," but I didn't have time for that. I had done plenty of missions without Link-16 and knew I could do this flight without it as well.

Unfortunately, the information it was providing was not reliable and only distracted me later in the flight. I got my jet back on line and out to marshal after a few minutes. I saw other event players taxiing for takeoff, and I sat anxiously waiting for my wingman. Just as I was about to taxi as a single, my wingman said he was "up." Unfortunately, during the taxi I noticed he had an intermittent auxiliary radio issue, and was forced to send him back to the line as a "down" aircraft.

Takeoff was uneventful, although now 25 minutes past my planned launch sequence time. I switched up to Desert Control who gave me the airspace for the event. The FRTC was now capped at 29,000 feet, a loss of over 10,000 feet of the planned altitude. After completing my G-warm, I climbed to 27K, my briefed rendezvous altitude. Turning to the primary strike frequency, I immediately heard the start of the roll call and I thought to myself "awesome, I made it!" At this point I was still in the west portion of the FRTC, but I gave my call sign accordingly when it was my turn.

I soon rolled up SEAD's tactical frequency and let the lead know I was down one ARM missile and I'd be a single for the event. The lead Growler rogered up my comm call with his call sign, and a discussion followed about how to service all the surface-to-air systems with the lack of my ARM missile. This is where I missed another opportunity to help avoid an impending mishap.

I should have proactively asked if there was any change to the game plan after the airspace had been capped. I did not. Instead, I elected to stay a silent wingman and believed that since I didn't get any new information upon checking in, nothing had changed. "Brief your flight, fly your brief," is what I grew up with, but applying this in a vacuum is what almost got me killed.

I missed yet another opportunity to ask about changes when I checked in with AIC (air intercept control). Due to crypto issues with the primary E-2C, I checked in with the backup controller "Bronco" and received only acknowledgement of my presence. Knowing this had become a flexed event, I should have proactively asked Bronco for any updates to the game plan, but failed to do so.

I was halfway thru the FRTC when "COMEX" (commence exercise) was called by the range training officer (RTO). Knowing I needed to ensure deconfliction between myself and an aircraft simulating a Standoff Land Attack Missile – Expanded Response

(SLAM-ER) profile, as well as the fighters pushing east to sanitize the air threat, I tried using Link-16 information to find the striker but noticed it was still degraded.

I biased to the north as best I could to stay out of his way and began to think about finding the strike package I was supposed to take separation off of. After having flown many of these events, I still wanted to sanitize my area with radar and confirm my rendezvous altitude was clear. After confirming there were no "hits" at my altitude, I entered the working area at 27,000 feet and rolled my radar down to try to find the strike package, which was briefed to be 1,000 feet below me.

After staying away from where I thought the simulated SLAM-ER missile aircraft was, I pushed down to the southern part of the airspace, skirting weather, and continuing to look for the strike package. I double-checked their planned altitude on my kneeboard card, and I tried to designate their Link-16 information without any luck. Thinking I was alone at 27K, I believed I was keeping a good inside/outside scan. I was wrong.

With an event which clearly wasn't going as planned, I should have verbally confirmed the location of the strike package and kept my scan level on the horizon vice biased to below me. Instead, as the push time approached, I started to look more underneath my aircraft for the strike package. Looking over my left canopy rail and down, I noticed a darker than sky spot in my peripheral at about the 10:30 level position.

I looked up and found myself on a 100 kt collision course with an EA-18G. Two things happened immediately. First, I was convinced I was going to die by having my canopy crushed by the Growler's wing pods and the bottom of its fuselage. I also started to put forward and right inputs into the controls in an initial attempt to fly the aircraft away. Second, I readjusted my flight path to see if I could avoid striking their cockpit with my left wing. I gently adjusted my stick inputs into the Growler in an attempt to get my wing below their cockpit and maybe, just maybe, clear their right wing and pods.

As I flew by the Growler I felt a movement in my flight controls very similar to employing a 500 or 1,000 pound bomb off of my left wing. I immediately looked over my right side and high and saw the other aircraft flying still at its original altitude as I was slowly descending. I looked at my left vertical stabilizer in my mirror and then at my left-wing and didn't notice anything visually wrong from my perspective. I then became concerned with descending through the stack and started to level off slowly. The Growler called a "knock it-off" over the strike common frequency, and I informed the RTO we had just had a midair.

The recovery of both aircraft was uneventful. Controllability checks were completed and both aircraft took precautionary traps. Relatively speaking, minimal damage was incurred and the mishap was ultimately labeled a Class B. My wingtip nicked the Growler underneath its cockpit. How simple it is to say, "Class Bravo " for monetary value, when just a few more feet or angle of bank could have ended in the loss of aircraft and life. I've had a great amount of time to reflect on this event, and will carry the experience with me for the rest of my life and career.

Despite my attempt at adhering to Admin and TacAdmin procedures, I failed to ask simple questions at critical points. I had bad situational awareness airborne, and missed the opportunities to correct it. We have been taught in our community to keep communication minimal and treat radio time as precious. However, when questions arise, staying silent is both counterproductive and dangerous.

What had been missed by not asking questions? Five minutes before I launched, the stack-game plan changed, and all players had moved down 2,000 feet in altitude from what was written on the kneeboard card. The Growlers' new rendezvous altitude was 27,000 feet and the strike package I was so concerned with finding was 3,000 feet below me, instead of 1,000. The new game plan was audibled but not rogered up by all players.

However, since everyone else was already up strike common, they at least heard the change where I did not. Although no one passed the change to me when checked in, with my experience, I should have known something was up.

Lessons Learned:

We learn from these events through articles, word-of-mouth, and through lessons learned. I hope my story reminds aircrew at all experience levels silence is not a solution, and a well-timed question can save the day. Naval Aviation is a dynamic environment and changes are bound to happen. However, when they do, aircrew need to slow things down and ensure they have the appropriate information to execute the event safely.

NOTES:

WHEN GOOD TANKING GOES BAD

F/A-18F SUPER HORNET, STRIKE FIGHTER SQUADRON ONE ZERO TWO (VFA-102) - DIAMONDBACKS

LCDR Kyle Vandegriff, Reported 2019

So there I was, on the wing of the KC-135 at night in southern Iraq with no way to tank. The tip of my refuelling probe had just been ripped off. This was most unfortunate. Let's take a step back and examine the series of events leading up to the loss of our probe and discuss how events unfolded during our divert to Al Asad Air Base.

This was my fourth flight in support of Operation Inherent Resolve (OIR) and was a night hop providing airborne electronic attack. I was no stranger to air operations in Iraq, having flown about 40 sorties in support of Operation New Dawn during the first EA-18G deployment in 2010-2011. In fact, I had been part of an expeditionary squadron that was based in Al Asad. During that deployment I learned some important lessons behind the tanker. Chief among those was: Always hang onto extra gas if you can, never make a play for the basket (because that's how things break) and avoid the Iron Maiden at all costs!

Tonight we were fragged for a seven-hour flight originating from and returning to our ship in the North Arabian Gulf. The tanking plan called for joining with the first tanker for a drag to our working area, followed by hitting a different tanker for our mid-flight gas and then a third tanker for a 45-minute drag out of country. All-in-all, my flight was fragged for a little over 40,000 pounds apiece. The weather was briefed to be cloudy up to 28,000 feet over most of western Iraq, with a cold front moving in from the west.

We met our KC-135 on time for the drag in-country. During the transit our jet had significant issues taking fuel into the external tanks. There was an outstanding gripe on the aircraft that called out a fuel transfer issue from the external tanks. Periodically fuel would just stop transferring, which would necessitate moving the appropriate external fuel switch to override (ORIDE) to get the fuel moving again. Tonight we had the opposite problem – fuel would not transfer into the tanks. We backed out of the basket and attempted plugging several more times, to no avail. Next, we backed out and moved the external tank switch to "stop" and back to "oride" several times before plugging again in earnest. At this point with no fuel in the external tanks, we were getting far enough from our primary divert that we needed to make a mission go/no-go decision. I flipped the external tank switch back and forth like a wild man and told my electronic warfare officer (EWO) I would give it "one more shot" before turning back and letting our wingman continue on the briefed mission. Lo and behold, we were finally able to get some gas into the externals, albeit slowly. Eventually we were able to top off and continued onto our primary tasking.

Mid-flight tanking on the Multi-Point Refuelling System (MPRS) went without a hitch, and the external tanks took gas like a champ. In accordance with the OIR baseline special instructions (SPINS) and good headwork we called up command and control (C2) 20 minutes prior to our fragged aerial refuelling (AR) time to check on the status of our tanker. We were informed that our fragged tanker was unavailable and we needed to transit to a new tanker in a different AR track 25 minutes away from our current location. This track was also 20 minutes in the wrong direction from the boat and our satellite divert, Al Asad. It took about five minutes to communicate this information to our wingman and get the flight rejoined.

As we started flowing southwest at 25,000 feet, we entered a standing cloud bank. The tanker was supposed to be at 26,000, so we sallied forth and waited to see what the weather ahead held for us. After checking in with the tanker, it became evident that they had climbed to 28,000 in the tanker track, looking for clear air. TAC C2 cleared us to 27,000 to join the tanker. Reaching 27,000, we were still in the clouds, so I elected to climb to 28,000 to get in clear air for the tanker join. As it turns out, the tops were between 28 and 29,500. However, the tanker was not permitted to climb above 28,000 due to airspace restrictions.

After some back and forth negotiation with the tanker, we were finally able to get them heading east, which allowed us to join on them and flow toward both better weather and the carrier for our scheduled recovery time. I screwed up the tanker join and wound up a mile in trail. This cost us fuel and time. As we were closing on the tanker they entered a solid cloud bank at 28,000. It was now about 10 minutes after our originally scheduled AR time.

Finally in port observation, we were cleared to the starboard MPRS pod. Prior to this my EWO informed me that it required 5,000 pounds of gas to get to Al Asad. I had not done a proper preflight divert fuel study for this area of Iraq, because I had not planned to be here. My EWO meant to communicate that departing the tanker with a 5.0 would get us on deck with a 2.3. I thought he was telling me that we would burn 5,000 pounds enroute to Al Asad. We were at about a 7.5. So to my thinking we had plenty of time... but not that much time.

The cloud we found ourselves in was quite turbulent. The only other time I had experienced this severity of turbulence behind the tanker was while tanking on a KC-135 MPRS north of Libya and they flew us into a thunderstorm. During that mission there was some loud clanging and banging on the refuelling probe due to turbulence, but it held fast. I had no reason to believe this time would be any different.

I stabilized behind the basket and noted that it was oscillating up and down what I estimated to be 8-10 feet at a time in a regular predictable cadence. My theory with MPRS had always been that if you can get in the basket with minimum drama, the rest is easy. My first approach to the basket had us climbing to meet the basket rather than driving straight and level. I backed away when I realized it wasn't going to work out. I started my second approach a little lower and drove straight in as the basket was moving from high to low. The probe made contact 1-2 inches at 2 o'clock from the bullseye. A small bit of nose influence and we made solid contact. No need to make a play for it.

Within two-seconds of contact, the basket had ripped away taking our probe tip with it. So much for my theory. Post flight tapes study revealed that we hit a pocket of violent turbulence at the same time we made contact with the basket. Because we had begun the approach slightly low the basket swung up and away from us, which I judged to be a good thing. In the darkness, it was immediately apparent that our probe had sheared. At this point, although surprised, we didn't waste any time departing the tanker and getting Al Asad on the nose. As the tanker once again cleared us for contact on the starboard pod, we informed our wingman via the boom frequency that we lost the tip of our probe in the basket and we were diverting to Al Asad.

Coming off tasking we had already spun Al Asad as the active waypoint. Because of the prior challenges taking fuel compounded by sketchy weather and a lower than desirable fuel state, my EWO had preemptively opened his divert pack to the appropriate page. However, the airfield frequencies in the divert pack that had been issued to us were woefully out of date. Luckily my EWO and C2 were on their game. We queried C2 for the current weather in Al Asad (clear) and the controller gave us all of the frequencies we needed. As briefed, we went through the entire ship to shore checklist to ensure that we would not miss anything on our approach to landing. Once everything was organized, I made a comment to my EWO to the effect of "well, sorry about all this, man." He responded with "Don't worry about that right now, let's just get the jet on deck." Excellent point! An American controller provided us with a Precision Approach Radar (PAR) to runway 09L. We executed the approach in a 30 knot right to left crosswind until just prior to touchdown.

The runway is quite long (13,000 feet) requiring minimal braking. However, the taxi light burned out during the landing rollout. With the probe already extended, the probe light did a great job of lighting our way once I slipped my night vision goggles on. Soon, a "follow me" truck met us and brought us to our parking spot. Thank you, Air Force!

Communications with our wingman indicated that the probe tip was not in the basket, as they were able to take fuel once exiting the cloud bank. Post-flight inspection revealed that the tip had been thrown free and had impacted the leading edge of our right vertical stabilizer, causing quite a bit of damage. True to its nature the Super Hornet airframe flew perfectly during the divert. A right engine inspection by maintenance personnel confirmed that no parts or pieces had been ingested into the engine. Still, we weren't going anywhere for a while.

Happy to be back on deck for now, we pulled circuit breakers after a long search for the APU's breaker, inserted pins and taped up all open orifices on the jet with the help of Air Force maintainers to prevent dust particulates from getting inside the aircraft.

After hundreds of hours flying the EA-18G, I was pretty disappointed by the turn of events. Still, there were some useful lessons I re-learned the hard way. If you're alive and breathing, then the situation you find yourself in is solvable and there is no need to go to general quarters. Slow is smooth and smooth is fast. That mentality could have been brought to bear with more intention during the last hour of our flight.

Lessons Learned:

A few lessons to consider:

Flying permanently as part of a two-man crew, it is easy to assume that you can split preflight planning duties. This is not the case. Each crew member should plan the entire flight as if flying alone. Only in this way will you consider the widest range of contingencies and plan appropriately for them. If I had done more thorough preflight divert planning, or if I had simply looked at my flight performance advisory system (FPAS) fuel on deck in Al Asad, I would have realized that we had plenty of time to let the turbulence die down a little before attempting tanking. Worst case, we could divert and recover aboard ship the following day.

- Nail the tanker join every time. The botched join forced us to pre-contact in turbulent weather when we could have done it in calmer, clear air with more gas in the tanks.

Make all communication as clear as possible, whether it is internal or external to the cockpit. Doing so would have improved our tanker join, ensured that the EWO and I were on the same page with respect to our divert fuel, and could have cut down on unnecessary internal comms during the divert.

NOTES:

COMBAT DIVERT: APPLIED CRM OVER THE SKIES OF IRAQ

F/A-18E SUPER HORNET, STRIKE FIGHTER SQUADRON EIGHTY ONE (VFA-81) - SUNLINERS

LT Alex Beasley, November 2019

The pressures of combat operations in support of Operation Inherent Resolve (OIR) can add an element of stress and task saturation to even the most seasoned aviators. But, sound execution of emergency procedures, the application of good headwork, and Crew Resource Management (CRM) - even in the face of perceived external pressures - can enable safe and survivable operations in a combat environment.

During a night combat sortie in the summer of 2018, Freedom 81 and 82, a flight of two F/A-18Es from the "Sunliners" of Strike Fighter Squadron (VFA) 81 and Carrier Air Wing (CVW) 1, launched from USS Harry S. Truman (CVN 75) and transited east for the evening's first tanking operation over Syrian airspace. It was the final day of planned combat operations before a well-deserved port visit, and VFA-81's most senior junior officer was leading the air wing commander on a close air support (CAS) mission. The thunderstorms they encountered along their ingress had given way to clear skies over the mission objective, and the flight was proceeding as briefed. While conducting in-flight refuelling, Freedom 81 received a full internal load of fuel but was unable to receive fuel in the center-line tank. After Freedom 82 received the fragged fuel, Freedom 81 elected to troubleshoot alongside the tanker. While troubleshooting, Freedom 81 received two cautions simultaneously, indicating low hydraulic pressure in his primary flight control circuits. Both cautions began cycling at approximately 10-second intervals. A quick scan of the hydraulic gauges revealed that the aircraft's Hydraulic 1 (HYD 1) pressure was cycling between 800 psi and 2200 psi, and per the Naval Aviation Training and Operating Procedures Standardization (NATOPS) manual, Freedom 81 secured the left engine. After securing the engine, Freedom 81 was unable to maintain altitude or airspeed and coordinated a descent to 19,000 feet via Tactical Command and Control (TAC C2).

Freedom flight was now faced with a dilemma. Due to thunder-storms along the egress route to the carrier, the return to friendly forces would require either a climb to high altitude or a lateral divert. Since operational restrictions limited any lateral deviation from the egress route, Freedom 81 had to decide between penetrating a thun-derstorm or diverting to an unfamiliar airfield miles away from the nearest U.S. maintenance support on the day before the carrier's planned move to the central Mediterranean Sea. After discussing their options, Freedom 81 and 82 decided that the primary divert airfield was no longer a viable option and elected to divert to Erbil, Iraq. On the transit to Erbil, Freedom 81 received multiple flight control system (FCS) cautions with degrades in the leading edge flaps (LEF) and rudder channels, as well as an amber flaps light indicating loss of normal function of the aircraft's flaps. Freedom 81 was able to clear the FCS caution with FCS resets for five minutes at a time. About halfway through the 200-mile transit to Erbil, Freedom 81 also received a fuel transfer caution. Freedom 81's feed tanks were indi-cating 1,500 pounds, while both the wing tanks and tank four were full. Freedom 81 and 82 conducted a thorough airfield discussion on their inter-flight frequency and developed a game plan to land the aircraft via a normal landing after restarting the left engine. Freedom 81 restarted the left engine 25 miles from the airfield and made an uneventful landing in Erbil. Freedom 82 landed and refuelled to make the flight's planned recovery time aboard Truman. Freedom 81 remained in Erbil for the next eight days, coordinating repairs and logistics for the rescue detachment.

Lessons Learned:

This incident taught the Sunliners and the CVW team some valuable lessons:

- Hydraulic System: After examining the aircraft, squadron maintainers discovered that a main hydraulic line in the HYD 1 system developed a one-inch gash. The location of the gash is a known issue in the Super Hornet, where the hydraulic line can rub against the generator control unit (GCU) and cause wear over time. Freedom 81's decision to secure the engine helped prevent the hydraulic pump from being destroyed and potentially causing a fire.
- Fuel System: Maintenance personnel also discovered that the tank three transfer pump had failed in flight. The tank three transfer pump is operated by the starboard engine, while the tank one transfer pump is operated by the port engine. By shutting off the port engine, the normally functioning tank one transfer pump lost its power source and stopped working. Fuel should gravity feed from tank four during these failure conditions, however, approximately 1,000 pounds per wing tank will not transfer without an induced side slip. In the case of Freedom 81's engine shutdown, fuel was not an issue, however, consideration should be given to the high likelihood of trapped fuel.

Freedom 81 faced real and perceived pressures in this scenario. Tasked with leading the air wing commander in combat, 81 dealt with deciding to divert to an unfamiliar airfield even though the aircraft carrier and all maintenance support would be steaming west later that evening. Complicated by bad weather, hostile ground forces and geopolitical constraints required all of the elements of the familiar DAMCLAS (decision making, assertiveness, mission analysis, communication, leadership, adaptability/flexibility, situational awareness) principles encompassed in CRM. A select few of these principles are highlighted below.

Assertiveness: Regardless of outside influences, compound emergencies require aircrew to assess the condition of their aircraft and make sound decisions that are critical to getting their aircraft safely on deck.

Freedom 81 and 82, in this case, had to apply an old axiom: "there is no rank in the cockpit (or flight)." By separating rank from the problem, a junior pilot was able to effectively handle a stressful inflight emergency and land without incident at an unfamiliar airfield at night. The cohesive teamwork demonstrated that evening was a direct result of the appropriate application of CRM principles in what could have been a very daunting environment for the junior officer.

Mission analysis:

This divert scenario presented an even greater external challenge since CVW-1, along with the rest of the Truman Carrier Strike Group, would be steaming west the following day and leaving its current operating area. Faced immediately with the knowledge that a major system casualty would likely lead to extensive delays on the deck while awaiting maintenance, Freedom flight had to apply the mission analysis portion of CRM. As the two pilots discussed their options, they arrived at the conclusion that, based on mission planning factors and the inability of the flight to return to the carrier safely due to poor weather and geopolitical limitations, the flight's best option was to divert east into Erbil. Of note, Freedom flight recognized in real time that maintenance logistics could pose an enormous challenge once on deck. They rejected this factor as insignificant and prioritized the safety of flight as the number one priority.

Adaptability/Flexibility: Arguably the most important CRM principle employed on this difficult mission was the adaptability and flexibility required to assess the situation, make informed decisions based on the best information available, execute sound NATOPS procedures and good headwork on the way to a successful divert. As tempting as it was to press west through questionable weather to avoid an unfamiliar divert scenario and a complex logistics problem, Freedom flight accurately prioritized the aircraft emergency and landed without further incident.

The intent here is to emphasize the importance of assessing in real time what the mission priorities are and reacting appropriately. Freedom 81's eventual return to Truman was a complex operation requiring major coordination with international and joint partners. In anticipating these difficulties, it might have been easy to succumb to "get-home-itis" and press a broken aircraft into a bad situation. Despite the challenges encountered, Freedom flight walked away from the flight having gained important experience on the value of applying sound CRM principles, even in the face of extensive perceived and actual operational stresses and challenges.

NOTES:

THE MOST UNDESIRABLE HIGH FIVE

E/A-18G GROWLER, UNIT WITHHELD

LT Ryan B. Ewanchew, December 2019

While embarked on deployment, my Electronic Warfare Officer (EWO) and I were up for a proficiency night flight with a sunset launch. We were approximately a month into deployment with flights averaging about one every other day. We were one of two Growlers launching in our event and coordinated to operate as singles during the event.

We performed a standard Naval Aviation Training and Operation Procedures Standardization Manual (NATOPS) brief following the pocket checklist and paying particular attention to the administrative portion of the flight.

Once we completed briefing the tactical and mission portion of the flight, we went to grab a quick bite before walking for the flight. As is standard on the aircraft carrier, the planes were parked with their wings folded in close proximity to one another. We arrived at the plane, receiving a standard brief from the Plane Captain (PC) in training, accompanied by his qualified PC. He verified all pins accounted for, the ducts were cleared, circuit breakers pushed in and we had the correct fuel load. We then shook the PC's hand and proceeded to get strapped into the aircraft after we performed our preflight inspection.

I did a quick sweep of the cockpit moving from right to left as I was connecting the last of my leg restraints and lap belt (Editor's note: In the E/A-18 interior checks checklist, the WINGFOLD switch should be checked to ensure it matches actual wing position to ensure there are no unintended wing movements after aircraft generators come online). Once we heard the announcement from Mini Boss to start Auxiliary Power Units (APU), we began to start the APU and then the right motor. The start was standard, but when the generators came online, I noticed more movement than usual out of the ground crew in my peripheries. My flight deck chief and plane captain were giving me the "fold wings" signal, but by the time I realized what they were trying to communicate to me, contact had been made.

The ALQ-218 wingtip pod (airborne electronic warfare system) struck the adjacent Growler's wingtip pod. I looked down to see the wing fold switch and confirmed it was in spread. The attempt to fold the wings failed, requiring the wing to be cranked to set it back to the upright position. After the wing cleared, the flight deck crew directed a shut down. Quality Assurance (QA) personnel began inspecting the damage to determine its extent, downing both jets in the meantime. All witnesses were required to give statements and execute the pre-mishap plan.

As soon as the wing crunch occurred, I felt a mixture of guilt and anger stemming from the internal questions I kept asking myself, "How could I overlook something so basic?" and "What was the cost in downed assets and parts to rectify this damage?" As the anger began to subside, I started to analyze how the situation manifested. I concluded that, from my point of view, this situation could have been avoided had I not taken things for granted.

Complacency is a basic issue within our line of work–even more critical on the flight deck of a carrier. It has the potential of being costly in loss of life or loss of equipment, preventing us from accomplishing our mission. That day, I failed to verify the position of the wingfold switch, and we paid for it with the downing of both Growlers for that wave and an indeterminate amount of time after that. I felt ultimately responsible as the pilot in command (PIC) and knew that more was expected of me.

'How could I overlook something so basic?'

Once maintainers inspected both planes, they determined that the only damage was a single drainage tube on the underside of the wingtip pod. The rest of the damage consisted of minor scrapes, which did not affect the structural integrity of the pods. One aircraft was back to full mission capable status by the next day and the other was awaiting a few more inspections to verify the integrity of the wing fold drive unit. Within two days, subsequent inspections found no additional problems with the other aircraft and it was back flying. Needless to say, the outcome was incredibly fortunate.

Lessons Learned:

The result was nothing short of a blessing, but we cannot look at this and say, "All is well that ends well." What we can do is take a step back to figure out what we can do differently to prevent this or another similar situation from happening again. As a squadron, we incorporated the addition of a wing fold switch, seat handle, master arm switch and anti-skid switch position into the plane captain brief to the aircrew. As aircrew, we are now confirming the wing fold switch position during our communication system checks before starting the fire warning tests. These measures will add a few more checks to prevent a situation in which personnel or equipment could be harmed or damaged.

Learn from my error and assess if complacency plays a part in your habit pattern so that you can identify it and take the appropriate steps to mitigate it.

I did not make the proper assessment of my habit patterns and was a part of the most undesirable high five I have ever been a part of in my life. We must keep each other safe on the flight deck or flight line and not let complacency lead us down the path of neglect and blunders.

NOTES:

THE DAY THE CABIN FLOW STOOD STILL

F/A-18F SUPER HORNET, STRIKE FIGHTER SQUADRON ONE ZERO THREE (VFA-103) - JOLLY ROGERS

LT Madison Pennington, December 2019

The environmental control system (ECS) throughout the F/A-18E/F and EA-18G community has been fraught with numerous systematic and operational malfunctions for many years. Lately, much attention has focused on a rash of hypoxic and decompression sickness illnesses caused by On Board Oxygen Generating System (OBOGS) faults and fluctuating cabin pressurizations throughout our community. While most of these occurrences have concluded with aircraft landing safely on deck, some have resulted in catastrophic and life threatening situations.

As wingman enroute to one of the local operating areas in eastern Washington state, my Electronic Warfare Officer (EWO) and I were focused on setting up our systems in preparation for a Suppression of Enemy Air Defenses (SEAD) training mission. About 20 minutes into the flight and level at 23,000 feet, I noticed the forward cockpit get eerily quiet and recognized a lack of cabin airflow through the vents. My personal checklist for any Environmental Control System (ECS) situation is to ask first: "Can we breathe?" Second, I ask, "Are we pressurized?" OBOGS was still working and the cabin pressurization was stable at the expected 8,000 feet.

Next, it was time to relay what was going on to my EWO. "I've lost airflow. ECS airflow. Confirm you have lost airflow?"

He replied, "Affirm, I've lost ECS airflow."

Being well outside normal operation for the system and not knowing whether we would possibly lose cabin pressurization, we decided to forego the mission, notify our lead what was going on, descend below 10,000 feet, and get the jet safely on the ground.

Funny thing about late winter in Washington – there is typically a cloud layer hovering low across the entire state. With a lack of self-contained precision approach capability, available airfield options become quite scarce on the eastern side of the mountains. After a brief conversation, we decided to take the jet west over the Cascade Mountains and back to Naval Air Station Whidbey Island. We received the clearance to take the lead and started coordinating with air traffic control for our new flight plan. In the descent passing through 11,000 feet, I felt a massive surge of airflow come through the vents with the built in test (BIT) page showing an environmental control system degradation alert (ECS DEGD).

A few moments later, I started getting a significant headache in my forehead and behind my eyes. Voicing the new symptom to my EWO, we acknowledged the possibility of hypoxia and executed the associated boldface. Our wingman coordinated a climb to get within radio range of squadron base and informed them of all events and our game plan and to activate the possible hypoxic event procedures. We elected to fly toward the local holding point to ensure all procedures and checklists were complete, and we were ready to land. Due to cloud layers, we commenced a precision approach radar (PAR), which degraded to a visual straight-in once below the weather. The emergency oxygen bottle lasted up until we turned to final – almost 20 minutes. Landing rollout and taxi were uneventful. Aviation medical determined that I was hypoxic and all applicable procedures were followed.

Lessons Learned:

The most notable strength and weakness during the flight was our tactical crew coordination (TCC) between the aircrew in our jet to our wingman. We effectively performed our procedures, developed a game plan and followed it through. Hindsight is 20/20, and we could have emphasized to our wingman that our checklists were completed and our intentions regarding section integrity once back to the local area. This additional crew coordination may have lessened our wingman's desire to "climb in our cockpit" and provide assistance. With that said, the adage "aviate, navigate, communicate" still applies. Take care of the proverbial "snakes in the plane," get the jet pointed where you want to go, execute checklists, let others know what is going on and how they can help, and return safely.

NOTES:

MY RIGHT OR YOUR RIGHT?
F/A-18E SUPER HORNET, UNIT WITHHELD

LT Brian Dallaire, December 2019

Our mission was a simple airways navigation flight from our home base of Naval Air Facility (NAF) Atsugi, Japan to the unfamiliar airfield of Marine Corps Air Station (MCAS) Iwakuni, Japan, as two sections of F/A-18E Super Hornets.

The weather that day was progressing worse than forecasted and we were forced to execute individual instrument approaches into MCAS. As we commenced our approach into Iwakuni, our initial concern was whether or not we would be able to effectively circle to land due to the low visibility. The minimums for the circling approach are a 520-foot ceiling and 1.5 statute miles of visibility. The field weather was reported as a scattered cloud layer at 1,500 feet and a broken layer at 2,200 feet with the visibility right at 1.5 statue miles and heavy rain. We were confident the instrument approach would get us below the layers, but the visibility was a bit disconcerting.

As I commenced the approach surveillance radar (ASR) approach, I was advised by the ground-controlled approach (GCA) controller that this would be an ASR to runway 02, circle to land to the east for a left downwind to runway 20. He requested a call advising him when I would be discontinuing the approach and executing circle to land procedures to the right for a left downwind.

Besides the heavy rain and turbulence, the approach was fairly uneventful. Around four nautical miles (nm) from the field, at 1,000 feet, the approach lighting system became visible. I continued following the controller's course corrections due to the poor visibility until the airport environment became clearer.

Around two nm, and just at approach minimums (550 feet), I advised the GCA controller that I was discontinuing the approach and making a right turn to circle to land. Approaching the threshold of runway 02 to my left, tower broadcasted over the GCA frequency that I needed to make a right turn to the left downwind for runway 20. Based on the voice inflection and urgency noticed in tower's transmission, I was immediately confused on which direction I was instructed to circle to land for runway 20.

With my only focus in the cockpit on keeping sight of the runway environment, the use of left and right in tower's instructions quickly became incredibly confusing. I began questioning whether or not I may have missed a radio call instructing me to circle to land to the west of the field rather than east -- the direction I was currently headed. I immediately requested that the tower verify the circling procedures, to which they simply repeated their previous transmission: a right turn for a left downwind.

Once again, the voice inflection suggested that my current location was wrong. Lacking assertiveness, I made the impulsive decision to respond to the tower that I was now turning left for a right downwind to runway 20. I hoped that the tower would now see either an incorrect turn to the downwind and immediately interject on my correction, or would remain quiet, indicating I was making a valid correction.

With no response from the tower, I was convinced that I had been instructed to circle west of the field and was now following their directions. It was not until I had already crossed completely over the runway, at the midfield point, that tower advised I was now circling in the wrong direction. They quickly instructed me to reverse direction, again, to try and circle to land to the east of the field. However, at this point, safety of flight became the ultimate priority, and I decided to land my aircraft. With a completely outside scan for obstructions of flight, as well as keeping the runway environment in sight, I advised the tower that I was initiating a right base for runway 20 and needed clearance to land. The tower immediately responded with clearance to land.

The right base pattern that I flew to touchdown brought my aircraft over Iwakuni at a very low altitude, inevitably causing concern for the local population below.

Lessons Learned:

By simply being assertive on my current location, as well as my intentions, I could have easily avoided an incorrect circling procedure in very undesirable conditions to an unfamiliar field. Although I felt rushed and crunched for time while executing the circling approach, by taking a few extra seconds to listen and comprehend what instructions the tower had given me, I could have analyzed and performed the correct procedures without hesitation.

NOTES:

IT WAS ONE OF THOSE NIGHTS
F/A-18E SUPER HORNET, OPERATIONAL TEST (OT-1) AND AIR TEST AND EVALUATION SQUADRON NINE (VX-9)

CDR Cade Hines, February 2020

Most of us have been there before. The last week of six weeks at sea, with no more no-fly days between now and the fly off. You're in the grinder, hoping the long busy days turn into a short week.

We had been at sea for the previous month in support of tailored ship's training availability (TSTA). TSTA went surprisingly well, and our crawl, walk, run approach seemed to be beneficial for the primary customer–the ship. The air wing also benefited greatly after having not been to sea much in over 18 months. Day and night cyclic operations, fuel planning, benign large force strike (LFS), moderate strike fighter weapons and tactics (SFWT) production and urban close air support (CAS) were all part of the daily routine. All in all, we were having a successful TSTA.

The ship pulled in to Norfolk for two nights to offload one fighter-attack (VFA) squadron and on-load the crew to support the first Operational Test (OT-1) of the F-35C Lightning II. The OT-1 team - people from VFA-125, VFA-101 and Air Test and Evaluation Squadron (VX) 9 - were all out to get some reps and sets with the F-

35C to see what lessons could be learned. What a great opportunity for everyone involved to be a part of this first for the Navy.

I felt proficient both day and night in and around the ship. The weather was typical for the area that time of year: night time thunderstorm buildups, but nothing too intense for our routine operations in the Atlantic. On the day of the event, I felt the slightest twinge in my throat. That could only mean one thing: after fighting it off for more than five weeks, I finally had "boat crud," just in time to jeopardize my spot on the fly off and bring home a cold to the family. Great. During flight briefing, the twinge had spread into a full-blown sore throat, but thankfully, other symptoms had yet to manifest. The flight I briefed was in coordination with three F-35s, four F/A-18E/Fs, two EA-18Gs, one E-2D, two MH-60Rs and was something I was very much looking forward to. By the time I walked, I had my first sniffle, but could easily clear my ears. I had no significant sinus stuffiness and my head felt fine.

I was at the jet early for my 11:15 p.m. launch. I chatted with the night check crew as much as any airman wants to chat with a 40-year old O-5, noted how spectacular the moon was (94 percent illumination, directly overhead), and enjoyed the breeze pushing across the deck while the ship made 28 knots.

It felt like it would be a great night.

As I walked around the back of the jet, I got a pretty healthy shower of jet fuel all over me, spewing out of some weep-hole on the aft starboard bulkhead during turn-around refuelling while I was checking the starboard wheel well. I typically could care less if I get fluids on my flight gear during pre-flight, but my oxygen mask was full of fuel. I tried to shake it out, and then used mask wipes to wipe it out enough to withstand the smell. As I used my last wipe, and gave it a test, the fumes and lingering smell of fuel was too much, so I had the ground crew go below deck to get another mask and hose. Meanwhile, I missed the event startups, and being parked on the four row on top of Cat 2, I knew a delayed start up would not be tolerated by the flight deck.

The replacement mask and hose arrived, and I fumbled around in the cockpit, trying to figure out how to secure the thing to the regulator. This took much longer than it should have, and only drove me to get more and more flustered. Eventually, I got everything secured, set up the cockpit for the start, and got the right motor online just in time to make the mass check-in on radio.

It was one of those nights.

The rest of the start up was nothing out of the routine, though I did need an identify friend or foe (IFF) crypto punch, global positioning system (GPS) punch, KY-58 punch, etc. At this point, you can imagine how flustered I was while a yellow shirt was waiting for the thumbs up to get me the hell off Cat 2! I eventually got it all done. The jet was fully mission capable (FMC) and ready to taxi. All that was left was to get the loaner mask adjusted and on while simultaneously taxiing, doing a hook check, aligning on the launch bar track, confirming the weight board and being hands up for arming.

Finally, I was airborne, and all was right with the world: a beautiful night and the jet was full up. Some puffy clouds on the base recovery course (BRC) during climb-out were easily visible due to the overwhelming cloud illumination. I was thrilled to be in the air and executed an unrestricted climb to 28,000 feet enroute to my combat air patrol (CAP) point. On the climb-out, I didn't notice any significant head, sinus or ear pain and was easily able to equalize above 8,000 feet. The mission itself was rewarding. My junior wingman and I had lots to observe and learn on this mission. We skirted some weather near our CAP point, but nothing serious. The other elements of the flight had significantly worse conditions to negotiate further out to the east, so we were pleased with the luck of the draw on this occasion.

At one point during the mission, our section was to execute an aggressive descent from 28,000 feet down to the deck and proceed inbound at high speed. We executed the profile without deviation, and it was here that I noted for the first time my inability to clear my right ear. While diving for the deck, I removed my mask several times in order to get a better grip on my nose, so I could better squeeze it while trying to equalize my ear pressure (Valsalva manoeuvre).

It took a few attempts, but in the end, I was able to just keep up with the pressurization schedule and achieve enough equilibrium to keep me from crying "Uncle." As you can imagine, trying to get that loaner mask on and off multiple times proved to be more challenging than it should, but that's what happens when you use gear that isn't yours. We completed our profile, executed our egress, and started a climb back up. This is when things went from nuisance to "uh-oh."

I had to level off our section in the teens as I now could not equalize the pressure in my right ear. I had lost most of the hearing in that ear just due to things being not-quite-right. I missed a couple of calls while trying to hear with my left, all the while trying feverishly to equalize the right with no luck. Eventually, the mission lead called the knock it off at the conclusion of the fight, which I heard and acknowledged, drove the section back toward the deck, fenced us out and checked in with Strike and Marshal.

During the hustle to get back to the ship on the last recovery, I was up to my ears in tasks, especially when the mission required a 120+ mile transit to CAP. During the shuffle and the subsequent descent while checking in with Marshal, I mis-heard the marshal radial, and dialled in the 300 instead of the 330. I set us up to descend away from the stack. It was only when I heard another section check in and their subsequent marshal instructions that I realized I had heard it wrong -- I had set our section up a good 25 miles from where we needed to be, with less-than-normal time to commence because of the last recovery, no launch requirement, ready deck.

It was one of those nights.

So, now I'm at 6,000 feet, the bottom of the stack, doing 525 knots, dodging thunderstorms, trying to shoot a point to point, while simultaneously valsalva'ing hard enough to blow air and snot out of my tear duct in my right eye!

It was one of those nights.

If there was any humor in the night, it came when I requested a Mode 1 approach, to which the controller replied, "Bullseye (approach guidance) is down."

Of course, Bullseye has nothing to do with a Mode 1 approach, so I replied, "Say status of Needles (Instrument Carrier Landing System)," to which I was told, "Needles unreliable." This will play into the story later.

But it was one of those nights.

I was able to get myself situated on the marshal radial with speed under control with about 45 seconds to spare. I knocked out a quick landing check list (HAIL-R), and commenced on time at the right spot. The approach and recovery, however, rocked my world. The physiological symptoms I encountered during the descent from 6,000 feet down to 1,200 were incredibly distracting. I tried a dozen times to get that right ear to equalize, but it was not having it and I elected to remain pressurized at probably 8,000 feet. Driving inbound at 1,200, I was chasing lineup from 12 miles in. "99, ship's in a turn..."

It was one of those nights.

"Bulleye is down, fly the final bearing... ship's in a turn, expected final bearing is..."

I feel like I missed my opportunity to fess-up somewhere between the eight mile dirty-up and tip-over, because I was struggling just to keep up with lineup while fumbling around trying to put on my mask. Eventually, I got automatic carrier landing (ACLS) lock-on, and of course, they were high and way right. By the time I got the lineup finalized, I was at tip-over and just figured I could muscle through the final 1,200-foot descent. I mean, how much worse could it get?

I'll go back to my previous reference to carrier air traffic control's (CATCC) characterization of Needles as "unreliable," and that was a fact. I'd surmise that between 3 miles and the ball call, ACLS lock was dropped 4-5 times. At a mile, I directed CATCC to "Stop locking me up," and then immediately called the ball. I'd say I was locked and dropped another three times during the last

20 seconds of the approach, and when flying PLM path, that produces the added symbology of the velocity vector appearing, and then disappearing, then reappearing and so on. As I was driving into the middle, paddles gave me a "little power" call, obviously seeing my settle at the start, wanting me to "fix my major malfunction." I adjusted the stick and placed the ship recovery velocity vector (SRVV) long until I saw the Meatball respond. From there, I relaxed pressure on the stick, tried not to go cross-eyed between the SRVV and velocity vector with out-to-lunch, non-corresponding Needles, and an ear that was still unresponsive to valsalva attempts.

The end result was a no-grade 1 wire, as you can imagine. And while that alone was humiliating enough, the subsequent taxi fam up the bow with that ear still bothering me had me ready to set the parking brake, kill the motors and slide down the flaps on the spot. "Uncle!"

Lessons Learned:

There's no point in writing all this if there were not lessons to be learned. In my scenario, there were many indicators that I could have used to readjust that night, if not pull the plug and cancel it all together. I've never had an issue with my ears, and if anything, I was more concerned with blowing out a clogged up sinus than being able to equalize ears. But, I should have terminated myself on that first aggressive descent during the mission, climbed to a comfortable altitude and then slowly worked my way down to an acceptable approach altitude.

Second, I should have better executed the first step of crew resource management (CRM), which is to properly communicate what was going on and perhaps differently task some of the section lead requirements in order to deal with the issue. As it was, I missed a call and ended up putting myself and my junior wingman in a disadvantageous scenario that might cause him to be late in marshal, or worse, get severely disoriented trying to make his timing such that he too has issues with the approach.

Finally, and most importantly, I should have talked to Paddles. When it came down to it, the rushed timing in marshal, the quick penetration and attempts at equalizing my ear, the weather encountered, the lack of bullseye, the turning ship and unreliable needles should have all led me to actually execute Carrie Underwood's million dollar plan of "Jesus Take the Wheel" by owning up to my degraded ability at five miles and saying, "Paddles, 300, I've got a bad ear and I could use a talk down, please." No harm, no foul, end of story. Those guys are there to save the day when you've done everything imaginable to screw it up.

While this story ended with a safe but humiliating 1-wire, many others have ended with catastrophic results. As a former Paddles, I used to relish the days when someone needed that extra nudge via some good bedside manner on button 15 or 17, and later came to tell a similar story about how things got all messed up during the flight, and they were grateful for the 9th inning save from Paddles. I should have called them in and worked the problem as a team, and not as an individual. Sorry, Paddles. Next time, I promise.

I met the doc in medical after my post-flight. He noted fluid had collected behind my ear drum and was trapped in my middle ear. Gave me some Afrin, Pseudoephedrine, and a down-chit with a note that said, "Take two of these and call me in the morning." It took all of the next day before I was finally able to Valsalva that ear back to sea level. The fluid subsided, the head cold passed, and the doc cleared me for the tanker drag cross-country five days later.

I regret my inaction in that flight, and hope that if you or your crew are in a similar situation where the odds are stacked against you, that you don't keep that secret, and let someone else with a different perspective contribute to the solution. Don't let it be one of those nights!

NOTES:

CHAPTER 4

LESSONS FROM PILOTS

*Lessons from P-51 Mustang Aircraft and Pilots
as flown in the movie, Top Gun: Maverick*

**"Overall, ensure that communication flows
between, aircrew, and mission planners to ensure
that we fly our aircraft safely and to their
maximum performance without accepting unnecessary risk that we bring on ourselves. Our
modus operandi is, "Fly, Fight, In".."**
LTJG Robert Kaplan
U.S. Navy

FEATURED AIRCRAFT

North American P-51D Mustang (featured in Top Gun: Maverick)

The American aviation classic, the P-51D Mustang takes its place amongst the latest U.S. Navy fast jets in the *Top Gun: Maverick* movie. It stars as Mavericks' own personal aircraft.

Tom Cruise is almost a real life Maverick as portrayed in *Top Gun*. It is rumoured that while filming the first movie he decided to obtain his pilot's license and eight years later he did just that in 1994. In real life, Cruise has said he is a multi-engine instrument-rated commercial pilot, able to fly both commercial airplanes and helicopters.

His most luxurious aircraft is his Gulfstream IV G4 private jet— costing around US$20 million, and capable of carrying 19 passengers. It travels up to 45,000 feet, and is equipped with a jacuzzi and a movie-screening room.

Cruise has always performed his own stunts, and having his pilot license for both airplanes and helicopters has definitely helped. He is able to fly almost anytime he likes. In the movie *Top Gun: Maverick* he flies the P-51D Mustang (but not the F-18E Super Hornet). It is not the first time on a movie that Cruise was able to climb into the pilot's seat, in both the 2017 movie *American Made*, and in 2018s *Mission Impossible: Fallout*, he performed his own stunts in a helicopter.

Tom's own Mustang is serial number 44-12840. Built in 1946, it was donated to a Civil Air Patrol unit, before ending up in an Illinois museum.

Completely restored by Art Teeters in 1997, Cruise purchased it four years in 2001. Renamed to *Kiss Me Kate* (after his ex-wife, Kate Holmes), it is stored at Valhalla Aviation in Los Angeles.

Nothing beats a P-51, so I wanted to include a number of lessons from P-51 pilots. So here are a few to ponder. Enjoy the learning. Blue Skies!

BUZZING THE PINERY
P-51D MUSTANG

Name Withheld, November 1998

Reporting pilot of the Aircraft #1 P51 Mustang, of a flight of 2, observed Aircraft #2 P51 Mustang doing aerobatics in Class B airspace and within the boundaries of an airway. In addition, when reporting in to home base tower, reporter #1 P51 Mustang, was accused of not contacting tower sooner before entering Class D airspace.

On the day in question, both aircraft departed Centennial with a prearranged prebriefed plan to form up after departing the airport area and to conduct formation flight ops. Having flown in formation for several minutes, it was agreed, via air-to-air com, that the aircraft would break formation and continue ops as single ships, to form up thereafter prior to returning to Centennial. Almost immediately upon breaking formation, Aircraft #2 commenced vigorous aerobatic manoeuvres, without first circling the airspace and, generally, in what was regarded by the pilot and pax in Aircraft #1 as op without regard to due consideration to safety, other aircraft in the area, and airway/controlled airspace. Aircraft #2 continued with an erratic and rather complete aerobatic profile for 20-30 mins, whereupon, at the persistent request of Aircraft #1, it finally reformed with Aircraft #1 in a loose formation, for return to Centennial airport.

Most of the aerobatic manoeuvres performed by Aircraft #2 were observed to have taken place in the vicinity of the Colorado Springs Airport, on the airway between Denver and Colorado Springs.

In preflight, Aircraft #1 had requested that Aircraft #2 maintain voice com with Aircraft #1 and appropriate ATC facilities at all times. Contrary to the briefing, Aircraft #2 did not do so.

Upon returning to Centennial in 'very loose' formation (with Aircraft #1 in contact with Denver approach, and contrary to direction from Aircraft #1), Aircraft #2 entered class B airspace without prior approval. Thereafter, Aircraft #2 was observed 'buzzing' the 'pinery,' a residential community just south of the Centennial Airport.

Following the low high speed pass over the pinery, Aircraft #2 abruptly pitched up and turned toward the Centennial airport. Most of the aforementioned occurred, at one time or other within the confines of class B and or C and or D and or E airspace (this is inclusive of the aerobatic and formation 'flying' attempted by the #2 Aircraft).

As the Aircraft approached Centennial on the return from the 'mission,' Aircraft #1, unable to evoke any response from Aircraft #2 prior to the latter's high speed low approach over the 'pinery,' advised Denver approach that he (Aircraft #1) would continue inbound as a single ship for landing at Centennial. Upon returning to Centennial, having been rather 'rattled' with this entire experience, and although I was handed off by approach to centennial Tower, the Tower suggested that I had not made 2-way radio contact with it, soon enough, prior to re-entering its airspace. In fact, I thought the tower had gotten quite 'testy' with me. I returned the favour with an 'exchange of words.'

Lessons Learned:

What I have relearned from this experience is, first, that the cockpit is no place for the resolution of disputes, particularly with ATC (such matters can and should be addressed at another time and place. For example, on the ground after the completion of the flight).

In this instance, I lost sight of these principles.

Candidly, I am ashamed of my lack of professionalism as a pilot, in having done so.

Secondly, and also in the relearned category, the wisdom of the axiom of never attempting formation flight with someone whose flying skills and attitude are unknown to you, was once again impressed upon me.

Although the foregoing might be viewed as relating principally to the ops of Aircraft #2, I am submitting this report out of concern that I might be viewed as having some complicity in, and/or responsibility for, said ops.

NOTES:

GEAR UP LANDING
P-51D MUSTANG

Name Withheld, May 1995

After total rebuild of a P-51D Mustang, I test flew it in the experimental category to show compliance for certification in the limited category. Upon lowering the gear for landing, I did not get a green light on the left-hand side. After exhausting all emergency procedures, a landing was made with very little damage.

After disassembly of left-hand gear actuator, it was found that some chrome had flaked off of the piston and galled the surface of the cylinder wall and pushed up a ridge of steel that the hydrolock pressure could not overcome.

The older P-51's had an aluminium piston that seems to work better.

Callback conversation with reporter revealed the following info: the reporter is a crop duster by trade and flies the P-51 and a Socata TBM in exhibitions. The aircraft is back in the air after 'very little' damage (port flap, port inboard gear doors, scrapes on the wingtip and scoop, and the tips of the prop blades). The prop blades have been trimmed and are still in use.

A Fargo FSDO (Flight Standards District Office) representative came to see the aircraft and rated this as an incident. He seemed to be more curious than anything. There was some question about a 'letter of authorization' being required to fly the aircraft.

Lessons Learned:

Know the history of your aircraft! Know the materials that used to be used, compared to what the engineers might have used as an 'upgrade'. Not all design changes are for the best!

NOTES:

AIRSHOW PERFORMANCE
P-51D MUSTANG

Name Witheld, September 1999

I was involved in a September 1999 airshow at Syracuse Hancock International Airport - a joint civil-military airport five miles north-east of downtown Syracuse, in Onondaga County, New York. For part of the airshow, the airspace was split and the airshow commenced on runway 33, situated north of runway 28, while commercial ops were occurring on runway 28. The FAA monitored briefing discussed how the airspace would be opened to include the entire airport, including the airspace over runway 28, when the P51 act commenced. It was also briefed that the airshow would have complete control of the airspace from the time the P51 act commenced until the conclusion of the airshow. During this briefing, I informed the airshow controllers of my need for the entire airspace and was informed by them that the entire airspace, including the airspace over runway 28, would be available for my act. As per the airshow briefing, I departed at approx. xx00. Shortly after departure, I was cleared into the entire airspace by the airshow control. I entered the airspace as briefed, overflying runway 28 at approx. 1,000 feet

AGL and approx. 5,000 feet down from the approach end of runway 28. As I was completing my first airshow manoeuvre at show centre (over the numbers of runway 15, north of runway 28), the airshow controller informed me that he had cleared me into the airspace too soon and asked that I hold until the airspace was available. I saw no aircraft during my entry to the airspace and over flight of runway 28, or at any time during this time frame, although I was later informed that a B727 was on final for runway 28. I was no closer than 5,000 feet horizontally and 1,000 feet vertically from this aircraft, based upon the reports I received.

Lessons Learned:

The next day the airshow rectified the situation by ensuring the waivered airspace included that over runway 28 before clearing the P51 into the airspace.

NOTES:

LOSS OF DIRECTIONAL CONTROL
P-51D MUSTANG

Name Withheld, April 1996

During a crosswind landing training at Ann Arbor Municipal Airport a wind gust was experienced on the rollout. The pilot under-corrected for the wind gust, with rudder and brakes, resulting in the aircraft departing the runway in a controlled manner at a shallow angle of attack.

The aircraft was accordingly slowed with a light coordinated application of the brakes for a turn back onto the paved surface. The largest angle of incidence to the runway centreline was less than 30 degrees. The aircraft did not ground loop and was within the pilot's control at all times except for the alignment change which was effected by the aircraft's right hand main landing wheel's contact with the turf.

Unfortunately, a runway edge marking light made contact with some part of the aircraft during the departure and was knocked down. The aircraft received no damage from either the contact with the light nor from the runway departure.

In preparation for this specialized tailwheel aircraft, the pilot initiated an intense training program for all predictable weather, and engine emergency conditions, covering the past 24 months.

The initial phase started with 65 hours in a Piper J3 Cub (dual and solo), advanced to 100 hours in a North American AT6 (dual and solo), and finished with 16 hours in a North American P51 Mustang equipped with a 2-place conversion with dual controls for final dual instruction.

Lessons Learned:

Training, training, training.

The solo training is ongoing and continues with an emphasis on simulated engine emergencies, landing gear deployment emergencies, and adverse weather conditions including various crosswind and gusty crosswind problematic sits. The pilot completed a biannual flight review in this aircraft in February 1996.

NOTES:

CHAPTER 5

FURTHER READING

There are a six other books in the *Lessons From The Sky* series. The goal of these books is to save as many lives as possible, and so there's something there for every pilot — fixed wing or rotary, military or civilian, private pilot or commercial:

51 Lessons From The Sky (U.S. Air Force)
61 Lessons From The Sky (Military Helicopters)
71 Lessons From The Sky (Civilian Helicopters)
72 Lessons From The Sky (Cessna 172)
81 Lessons From The Sky (General Aviation)
101 Lessons From The Sky (Commercial Aviation)
Top Gun Lessons From The Sky (U.S. Navy)

I WOULD REALLY APPRECIATE if you could post a review (or simply a rating) online. Your review may help save the life of another pilot.

Blue skies.

GLOSSARY

U.S. Navy & Aviation, Acronyms, Terms, Assignment, Rank, Units and Facilities

The U.S. Navy uses a number of specific acronyms to indicate important information in an efficient manner. By establishing acronyms that symbolize important phrases, Navy personnel can share information faster and be more precise with a standardized vocabulary.

1v1 - **One versus One** - Dogfighting
1v2 - One versus Two - Dogfighting one on two
A-LOC - Almost G-induced Loss of Consciousness. Nearly passing out due to lack of blood in the brain as a result of pulling G's.
A/A - Air-to-air. An aerial fight between two or more aircraft.
A/S - Air-to-Surface. A general term for the missions and/or equipment involved in the aerial attack of surface (land or sea) targets.
AAA - Anti Aircraft Artillery
AARGM - Advanced Anti-Radiation Guided Missile

ACLS - Automatic Carrier Landing System

ACM - Air Combat Manoeuvring

ACMR - Air Combat Manoeuvring Range

ADC - Air Data Computer

ADM - Admiral

AFCS - Automatic Flight Control System. The computer-directed system that accepts a pilot's flight control inputs, then factors in current pitot static and aircraft information before deflecting flight control surfaces.

AFFF - Aqueous Film Forming Foam

AFM - Airplane Flight manual

AGL - Above Ground Level

AIC - Air Intercept Control

AJB-3 - Attitude sensor, Bombing Computer

AME - Aircraft Maintenance Engineer

Angels - Height of an aircraft in thousands of feet

AOA - Angle of attack

AOW - Auxiliary-man of the Watch

APU - Auxiliary Power Unit. A small jet engine used to provide aircraft systems power (hydraulic, electrical, etc.).

ARI - Aileron Rudder Interconnect

ASAU - Air Search and Attack Unit

ASR - Approach surveillance radar

ASUW - Anti-surface Warfare

ASW - Anti-submarine Warfare

ASW - Auxiliary SeaWater System

ASWO - Anti-Submarine Warfare Officer

ATC - Air Traffic Control

ATFLIR - Advanced tactical forward looking infrared

AUTEC - Atlantic Undersea Test and Evaluation Center

AUX - Auxiliary

AWACS - Airborne Warning and Control System

BALD - Bleed-air-leak detection

Bandit - A known *bad* guy

BFM - Basic Fighter Manoeuvres. Aerial manoeuvres employed during ACM Air Combat Manoeuvring, aka Dogfighting. Close-quarters A/A combat where each pilot tries to shoot down the other, preferably first.

Bingo - Low fuel status or direction to head for the divert Field

BIT - Built in Test

BMOW - Boatswain's Mate of the Watch

Bogey - An unknown radar contact

Bolter - An aircraft fails to catch an arrestor cable

BOQ - Bachelor Officer Quarters

BRA(A) - Bearing Range Altitude (Aspect). The format of an air intercept communication call when referenced to the fighter position.

BRU - Bomb Rack Unit. An adapter housed in an aircraft weapons pylon that supports the loading and wiring of various A/S Air-to-Surface racks, rails, launchers, and munitions.

Bug - Exit a dogfight rapidly / bugging out

BUPERS - Bureau of Naval Personnel

CADC - Central Air Data Computer

CAG - Commander, Air Group - An obsolete but more-easily spoken term for CVW Carrier Air Wing. A U.S. Navy aviation organization composed of approximately eight independent squadrons that join as one team when deployed aboard an aircraft carrier. Also, informal title for the CVW Commander, typically a U.S. Navy Captain (O-6).

CAP - Combat Air Patrol

CAPT - Captain

CAS - Close Air Support

CATCC - Carrier Air Traffic Control Center Certifications

CATM-9X - Captive Air Training Missile, AIM-9X weapon system

CATMs - Captive Air Training Missile. An A/A missile used for training that lacks many, or all, of the components found on live missiles.

CAVU - Ceiling and Visibility Unlimited

CCA - Carrier Control Area

CDR - Commander

CFITs - Controlled Flight into Terrain

CO - Commanding Officer

COLD CAT - With steam catapults, "cold cat" is a specific term to describe a specific failure that results in the aircraft not obtaining the desired speed

COMEX - Commence Exercise

COMNAVAIRPAC - Commander, Naval Air Forces, Pacific

COMNAVSEASYSCOM - Commander, Naval Sea Systems Command

COMNAVSECGRU - Commander, Naval Security Group

COMPACFLT - Commander, Pacific Fleet (formerly CINCPACFLT)

COMPEX - Competitive Exercise

COMPTUEX - Composite Training Unit Exercise

COMSEC - Communications Security

COMSUBLANT - Commander, Submarine Force Atlantic

CONUS - A technical term used by the U.S. Department of Defense and others, has been defined as the continental United States.

CPO - Chief Petty Officer

CQ - Conditionally Qualified

CRM - Crew Resource Management

CRT - Combat-rated thrust

CV - Aircraft Carrier

CVIC - Carrier-Based Intelligence Center

CVN - Aircraft Carrier Nuclear Propulsion

CWO2 - Chief Warrant Officer Second Class

CWO3 - Chief Warrant Officer Third Class

CWO4 - Chief Warrant Officer Fourth Class

DACT - Dissimilar Air Combat Training

DAPA - Drug and Alcohol Programs Advisor

DCA - Defensive Counter Air. An A/A mission where fighters reactively engage an adversary, typically over neutral or friendly territory, in the defense of some protected asset(s).

DCAG - Deputy Air Wing Commander

DCC - Damage Control Central

DCM - Defensive Counter Measures

DCO - Direct Commission Officer

DDI - Digital Display Indicator

DE - Destroyer Escort

DEGD - Degraded

Delta Sierra - A military acronym from the Vietnam war era. It stands for "DS", which is how military personnel would describe a bad situation, or poorly planned mission. It stands for "dog shit."

DESDIV - Destroyer Division

DEVGRU - Naval Special Warfare Development Group

DFS - Dynamic flight simulator

DL - Destroyer Leader

DLGN - Nuclear Powered Guided Missile Destroyer Leader

EAT - Estimated Arrival Time

ECM - Electronic Countermeasures

ECS - Environmental Control System

EMCON - Radio silence or Emissions Control

ENS - Ensign

EPs - Emergency Procedures

EWO - Electronic Warfare Officer

FADEC - Full Authority Digital Engine Control

FADM - Fleet Admiral

FAST - Fleet Air Superiority Training

FCLP - Field Carrier Landing Practice

FFARP - Fleet Fighter ACM Readiness Program

Firewall - Push the throttles to their forward limit

Flogger - NATO reporting name for Mikoyan-Gurevich MiG-23

FLXXX - Flight Level

FMF - Fleet Marine Force

FMSS - Field Medical Service School

FNAEB - Field Naval Aviator Evaluation Board

FOD - Foreign Object Damage (Debris and Detection also used in some cases)

FPAS - Flight-performance-advisory-screen

FRS - Fleet Replacement Squadron

FRS - Fleet Replacement Squadron (Formerly **RAG**)

G - Gravitational Force. The pull of earth's gravity that people and objects experience as "one G" in an unaccelerated state or "zero G" when falling.

G-LOC - G-induced loss of consciousness

GBU-16 - Laser guided bomb

GCA - Ground-Controlled Approach

GCU - Generator Control Unit

GQ - General Quarters (Call to battle stations)

HAC - Helicopter Aircraft Commander

HEFOE - Hydraulic Electrical Fuel Oil Engine. A term used with associated numbers (1 for H, 2 for O, etc.) to convey aircraft malfunctions via hand signals between aircrew when radios are unavailable.

HELO - Helicopter

HM - Hospital Corpsman

HS - Helicopter Squadron (HS-4 Black Knights)

HSI - Horizontal situation indicator

HUD - Head Up Display

HYD - Hydraulic

ICLS - Instrument Carrier Landing System (Needles)

ICS - Intercommunications System

IFF - Identify friend or foe

ILS - Instrument Landing System

IMC - Instrument Meteorological Conditions

IMER - Improved Multiple Ejector Racks

IMN - Indicated Mach Number

IP - Instructor Pilot

IUT - Instructor Under Training

JBD - Jet Blast Detector (carriers)

JLASE - Joint Laser Systems Effectiveness

JP-5 - Military jet fuel

JTAC - Joint Terminal Air Controller

JTAC - Joint Terminal Attack Controller

JTF - Joint Task Force

JTFEX - Joint Task Force Exercise

Knock-it-Off - Directive to all aircraft to cease manoeuvring

LCDR - Lieutenant Commander

LES - Leave and Earnings Statement

LFS - Large Force Strike

LPO - Leading Petty Officer

LSO – Landing Signal Officer (Paddles)

LT - Lieutenant

LTJG - Lieutenant Junior Grade

MCAS - Marine Corps Air Station

MCPO - Master Chief Petty Officer

Midrats - Midnight Rations. Food that is served at or around midnight for the shift either coming onto or being relieved from a watch.

MiG - Mikoyan-Gurevich (designer of Soviet aircraft)

MM - Machinist's Mate

MO - Maintenance Officer

MOVLAS - Manually Operated Visual Landing Aid System

MPRS - Multi-Point Refuelling System

MRT - Military Rated Thrust

MSC - Military Sealift Command

MSL - Mean Sea Level

MSW - Main Seawater System

NAF - Naval Air Facility

NAS - Naval Air Station

NATO - North Atlantic Treaty Organization

NATOPS - Naval Aviation Training and Operation Procedures Standardization Manual

NAVAIR - Naval Air Systems Command. A U.S. Navy organization whose mission is to provide full life-cycle support of naval aviation aircraft, weapons and systems.

NAVPRO - Naval Plant Representative Office

NAVSUP - Naval Supply Systems Command

NAVTRA - Chief of Naval Training

NAWCWD - Naval Air Warfare Center, Weapons Division (now Pacific Missile Test Center)

NBSD - Naval Base San Diego

NCDU - Navy Combat Demolition Unit

NCIS - Naval Criminal Investigative Service

Needles - ICLS, Instrument Carrier Landing System

NFO - Naval Flight Officer

No Joy - No visual confirmation of another aircraft (especially an enemy) has been made

NVAF - North Vietnamese Air Force

OBOGS - On-Board Oxygen Generation Systems

OCF - Out of Controlled Flight (aka "departed" flight) the jet is tumbling out of control

ODO - Operations Duty Officer

OIR - Operation Inherent Resolve

OOCF - Out-of-control-flight

OOD - Officer of the Deck

OPNAV - Office of the Chief of Naval Operations

OPNAVINST - Chief of naval operations Instruction

OPSO - Operations Officer

OPTAR - Operating Target

Paddles - LSO – Landing Signal Officer

PADS - Position, altitude, distance and speed

PAR - Precision Approach Radar

Parted wire - A cross-deck pendant (aka "wire") breaks as an aircraft lands

PCL - Pocket Checklist

PID - Positive Identification

PLAT - Pilot Landing Aid Television. A system of low-light TV cameras and displays positioned as a tool for, and to record, aircraft carrier landings and flight deck operations.

PO - Petty Officer

PO1 - Petty Officer First Class

PO2 - Petty Officer Second Class

PO3 - Petty Officer Third Class

POOW - Petty Officer of the Watch

PRIFLY - Primary Flight Control (Aircraft carriers)

PSNS and IMF - Puget Sound Naval Shipyard and Intermediate Maintenance Facility

PT - Physical Training

Punch out - Eject from an airplane

QA - Quality Assurance

RADALT - Radar Altimeter

RADM - Rear Admiral

RAG - Replacement Air Group

RAMP events - Occurrences during, or as a result of, ground handling operations

Ramp strike - A landing aircraft is so low it hits the back of the ship (usually catastrophic)

RIO - Radar Intercept Officer

RL - Restricted Line Officer

RMD - Restricted Manoeuvring Doctrine

RMI - Radio Magnetic Indicator - the card of the RMI acts as a gyro-stabilized magnetic compass, and shows the magnetic heading the aircraft is flying.

ROBD - Reduced Oxygen Breathing Device

ROE - Rules Of Engagement

Roger - Based on then-use of the given name Roger in the phonetic alphabet for the word for the letter R. The Roger stands for the initial R in "(Message) Received."

RPM - Revolutions per minute

RTC - Recruit Training Command, Great Lakes, Illinois

RTO - Range Training Officer

SA - Situational Awareness

SAM - Surface to Air Missle

SAR - Search And Rescue

SCBA - Self-contained Breathing Apparatus

SCPO - Senior Chief Petty Officer

SCW - Seabee Combat Warfare Specialist Insignia

SDO - Squadron Duty Officer. A squadron aviator who assists the **ODO** during execution of the flight schedule.

SEAD - Suppression of enemy air defense

SECDEF - United States Secretary of Defense

SECNAV - United States Secretary of the Navy

SFARP - Strike Fighter Advanced Readiness Program

SFWT - Strike Fighter Weapons and Tactics

Sierra Hotel - A term used by fighter pilots (and those who want to be), meaning "Shit-Hot"

SIR - Streamlined Incident Report

SLAM-ER - Standoff Land Attack Missile – Expanded Response

SLBM - Submarine-launched Ballistic Missile

Sliders - Miniature hamburgers. The name originated in the 1940s, when sailors in the U.S. Navy would refer to mini-burgers as "sliders" because of their extreme greasiness.

SN - Seaman

SOP - Standard Operating Procedure

SR - Seaman Recruit

SRVV - Ship Recovery Velocity Vector

TAC - Tactical Command

TACAN - Tactical Air Navigation System

TACTS - Tactical Aircrew Combat Training Systems

TAD - Temporary Additional Duty

Tallyho - Shortened to "Tally" - Enemy in sight - adopted by U.S. military pilots during WWII, from British fighter pilots, who in turn had adopted it from fox hunting.

TCC - Tactical Crew Coordination Procedures

TDC - Target Designator Control

TF - Task Force

TG - Task Group

TIT - Turbine Inlet Temperature

TOPGUN - United States Navy Fighter Weapons School

TOT - Target On Time

TSTA - Tailored Ship's Training Availability

TU - Task Unit

UHF - Ultra High Frequency

URL - Unrestricted Line Officer

USN - United States Navy

USNA - United States Naval Academy (Annapolis)

USS - United States Ship

VADM - Vice Admiral

VDI - Vertical Display Indicator

VFA - Fixed Wing Fighter Attack Squadron

VFR - Visual Flight Rules

Visual - Means friendly in sight

VMC - Visual Meteorological Conditions

VP - Fixed Wing Patrol Squadron

VRC - Fleet Logistics Support Squadron (VRC-30 Providers)

VSI - Vertical Speed Indicator

VTU - Volunteer Training Unit

WAVE OFF - A mandatory order to abort the landing and go around for another attempt.

WESTPAC - Western Pacific Deployment

Wingman - A pilot who supports another in a potentially dangerous flying environment. Wingman was originally the plane flying beside and slightly behind the lead plane in an aircraft formation.

WO - Warrant Officer

WO1 - Warrant Officer First Class

WSO (Wizzo) - Weapon Systems Operator/Naval Flight Officer

WTD - Watertight Door

XO - Executive Officer is second in command to the **CO**

ACKNOWLEDGMENTS

I wish to thank these few people who have helped me with this very specialised book of lessons. Whether they realise it or not, our conversations or our serious chats, and the discussions around military flying, really helped me finish this book. Thank you.

Paul 'Simmo' Simmons AM CSM
Scott 'Macka' McKenzie
E. Vincent 'Jell-O' Aiello
Dave 'Bio' Baranek
Warner 'Warns' Cowin

As I think of all the people who have influenced my television production and writing career, it is incredible to see the support and helpfulness of just one person. Thank you Kirsten McKenzie. I appreciate your time and effort in helping me.

ABOUT THE AUTHOR

With a passion for aviation passed on from his father who worked in the National Airways Corporation (NAC) office in Auckland, New Zealand. Fletcher often heard about the NAC DC3 Kaimai Ranges crash, this had made an impact on his father as he knew one of the flight attendants killed in the accident.

As a teenager, Fletcher knew the youngest instructor on his first gliding course who was sadly killed in a glider crash some months after that course.

Over his flying carrier, and during his adventures filming extreme aviators around the world, the deeper Fletcher read into understanding the situations pilots got into, and the more he understood the factors might lead to poor decision making in the skies above.

Coupled with twenty years of experience working with global entrepreneurs through EO (Entrepreneurs Organisation), training them to experience share between each other and to learn from any mistakes, Fletcher selected and compiled these stories to help us learn from others. To ensure current and future pilots will be safe in the skies.

www.fletchermckenzie.com

Printed in Great Britain
by Amazon

40032208R00155